A Few Things I've Noticed

Enjoy!

Madora Kibbe

A Few Things I've Noticed

Madora Kibbe

iUniverse, Inc.
New York Lincoln Shanghai

A Few Things I've Noticed

iUniverse, Inc.

For information address:
iUniverse, Inc.
2021 Pine Lake Road, Suite 100
Lincoln, NE 68512
www.iuniverse.com

Portions of this book first appeared in substantially the same form in The Christian Science Monitor, The Review Press and The Villager.

ISBN: 0-595-31416-3

Printed in the United States of America

For my Dad, and for Miranda

Contents

Mothers and others

A few things I've noticed

Foreword

Readers of The Christian Science Monitor have known for years what you may be about to discover: that when you see "Madora Kibbe" at the end of an essay, you're in for a rare treat. It's a humorous, witty, honest and heartfelt treat. Can a treat be touching, too? These treats are. Whether she's writing about a dog that thinks he's a human, the real reason she wants her daughter to play field hockey, or why children's artwork is so precious, Madora Kibbe never fails to engage and entertain. She's like a welcome guest who can only stay a moment but gives you her full attention and leaves you refreshed and—more than likely—laughing. Her topics are rooted in the everyday of her life at the moment: motherhood, school, the suburbs. But her voice and wry outlook are far from ordinary. She's part stand-up comic, part reporter, part poet—but a poet who's not above penning humorous verse.

One more thing about the next to last essay in this collection: As newspaper editors across the country will tell you, the terrorist attacks of 9/11 sent a tidal wave of essays pouring into every newsroom. By far, most of them failed to come to terms with the enormity and the emotion of that day. Madora Kibbe's essay did. She surprised me. The wellsprings of her art—her family, her marriage, her children—provided an abundant source for her to deal with those events in a way that is spare, poignant; and consoling.

So, prepare to be surprised, as well as delighted and amused. And don't say you haven't been warned.

Owen Thomas
Editor, The Home Forum
The Christian Science Monitor

Acknowledgments

I need to thank a plethora of people for helping me put this book together. Steven Schnur for teaching by shining example how to be a writer. Judy Richter, Diana Asher, Eleanor Hoenig and all the other members of the Sarah Lawrence Writers Institute Fiction Writing class for listening and laughing and criticizing gently.

This book is all about my family and friends and the town that I live in and I am deeply grateful to all of them, especially my children, for their allowing me to describe them in such mostly kind but certainly microscopic detail.

The AKA Writers—Linda Howitt, Hondi Brasco, Laura Edwards, Cynthia Beglin, Liz Folberth, Skip Mechlin and Janet Stampfl are my team mates in this wonderful wacky world of combining authorship with a home life.

Thank you Owen Thomas for being what every writer needs—a really good editor. And a really good friend. Thank you Maggie Lewis Thomas my permanent pal and former editor who's always just a phone call away whenever I need encouragement or a nice cup of tea.

But the one I want to thank the most is my best friend, fact checker, steadfast supporter, my husband Jon.

Kids

Why children's artwork is so precious

Our children go to a progressive school, which I'm beginning to think means a school that will progressively drive their parents out of their minds. They are in the second grade, but neither of them has a desk. They have tables that they share with other classmates. They have work stations. They have the carpeted floor to lounge on during something called "meeting." But for all the tax dollars we ante up semiannually, neither of them has a—you know—desk.

Don't get me wrong; I love our kids' school. But this one little,—what shall I call it? Quirk—irks me. This is not my vision of elementary school. How will they master organizational skills, or have a sense of their own private space? More important, how will they pass notes to friends, or whisper across the row, their heads under their desktops, while they pretend to search for a lost ruler? They will not, they cannot, because they have no desk.

Our children are in different classes, with different teachers, because they are twins and twins are always separated at this very progressive school. Believe me, this is a good thing; twins see enough of each other at home. But because our kids are in the same grade, they often have the same homework assignments. Back in October, they both brought home an assignment sheet that loudly proclaimed in boldface letters CHILDREN'S ARTWORK IS PRECIOUS! True, I agreed, thinking that there's nothing more precious than a little math homework, however.

But no, there was no math to be done, at least not this time. Instead, our children were to create, on their own, the assignment sheet warned, a Halloween haunted house. Fine, my husband and I thought, let them pull together two little houses of their own devising. It'll be fun, I guess. I have always expected that I would assume a hands-off approach to my children's homework assignments.

I would stand by, on guard and ever ready, but I would never, ever be one of those meddling, manipulative moms who actually got involved with their children's work. Not me. I was above that sort of thing, mainly because I always figured I'd have as much interest in participating in a child's art assignment as I would in learning how to play bridge, which I place on a par with driving into Queens to purchase curtains, which only an idiot would do. I am many things, but not an idiot. No Queens, no bridge, no artwork. When it came to haunted houses, they were on their own.

And they each did a very nice job and turned in houses that looked as though they were made by seven-year-olds. Our daughter made a haunted schoolhouse out of an old box that previously held books. (Soon I will steal back her haunted schoolhouse and repack it with books.) Our son made a haunted home out of a shoe box. These were modest, heartfelt offerings. They were also completely out-classed by most of their peers, who arrived at school toting five-foot, massive mansions, some involving knowledge of electrical wiring. Some had sound effects. Some had blinking lights. All were carried in by blushingly proud parents.

The minority of us who had stuck to the assignment were shocked. So this is the true meaning of Halloween: parental one-upmanship. Still, my husband and I patted ourselves on the back, acting smugly self-righteous. We would never slide to such a low level; we would take these assignments seriously. Privately, we felt like, yes, idiots. The children were oblivious. They couldn't seem to tell a child-made house from a grown-up one. They were simply delighted that the hall outside their classrooms was now crowded with somebody's—anybody's—precious artwork, which could only mean that Halloween was just a shout away.

So when the next assignment came home, trumpeting once again that CHILDREN'S ARTWORK IS PRECIOUS! and that the children were now supposed to create a holiday decoration, my husband and I sniffed and snorted and swore that we would not stoop to the petty echelon of those Other People. Oh no, this was to be an independent project once again. The kids were to pick out their own holiday symbol, anything from a crèche to a dreidel to a candy cane. Our daughter decided on a papier-mâché snowman. Well, I thought, at least I can help her make the flour-and-water paste, maybe help tear the newspaper into strips. But after that, she's on her own.

Our son chose to construct a miniature fireplace, complete with tiny Christmas stockings hanging down. He found an even smaller box this time and set out to design his creation. My husband saw him fiddling with a few sticks and promptly went out back and chopped miniature logs for him to place in the front of the box. Our son found some gray packing material and fashioned a chimney out of it. You need a mantle, my husband said. What's a mantle? our son asked. The next thing I knew, the two of them were hammering something in the basement, and when they came back upstairs the box had a wooden mantle, with perfectly spaced nails for hanging the stockings.

But I didn't pay much attention to what they were doing. I was too busy wrapping papier-mâché strips around the snowman's head. "Can I do some, Mommy?" Our daughter asked politely. "In a minute," I replied. Later, we suggested purchasing small woolen stockings for our son to hang from the nails on his mantle, but he said he really preferred the little red ones he had cut out of paper. And our daughter didn't want the fur hat her grandmother offered to donate to the snowman. For some reason, she wanted to make one out of construction paper, too.

Then disaster struck. Somehow, some way, our daughter's snowman was thrown out. I don't know how this happened—maybe someone mistook it for, dare I say it, garbage? We made this discovery at 5:30 Sunday afternoon. The assignments were due the following day. Springing into action, my husband proclaimed we'd make a papier-mâché star! "Huh?" we all said in response. Why not another snowman? But no, his eyes were dancing with inspiration. He took wire hangers and, like some suburban Calder, fashioned them into a five-pointed hanging celestial body. This we covered in papier-mâché and spray painted gold. Then our daughter dabbed orange dots all over our perfect gold star. It was difficult to restrain ourselves, but in the end we let her do it. After all, it was her project.

None of the other children seemed to notice any qualitative difference between our children's Halloween projects and the Christmas ones, but we know their parents did. Very few children were allowed to do their own artwork this time around. I'm guessing Valentine's Day will be the Grand Prix of art events. I was thinking of hiring a harpist, but my husband says we'll never find one willing to play inside a fountain. Especially one that blows bubbles. And now I know why, truly, children's artwork is so precious. Because it is so very, very rare.

Beautiful music,
bad notes and all

He'd only had six lessons. He's only six years old. Still, our son was committed to taking part in his first piano recital. He exudes that "can do" attitude so often found in kindergartners. Never mind the fact that everyone else involved in the late-spring concert had been playing since September, at the very least. But the piano teacher seemed to feel our son was up to the task, and apparently so did he. He chose two pieces. He played them well, as well as one can play "Old Mac-Donald," described on the program as "Traditional," and "Mary Had a Little Lamb," described as "Folk Song." Apparently, no one wants to take credit, or blame, for either of these fine selections. And when I say he plays them well, what I mean is he plays all the right notes and in the right order, too. There's not much to interpret. There is no subtext at this stage of the game.

Since it was his first-ever recital, I thought I'd better sit in on the dress rehearsal the day before, to get a feel for what was in store. I was the only adult present—other than the piano teacher, who had to be there. The other parents dropped and ran. I was there as an advance man to scout out the doings for the rest of the family, to let them know just how bad the whole event was going to be.

"Bad" is such a relative term. In some contexts, "bad" can even mean "good." Alas, this was not that context. This was children ages 6 through who knows what; I'm not a good judge after age 10. Maybe they were all young and some were just very tall. Remember Prof. Harold Hill's "think system" in the movie "The Music Man"? This was somewhat better than that. What these kids lacked in artistry they made up for in brevity. And they all knew how to bow very well.

But perverse parent that I am, the worse it got, the more I liked it. For one thing, my son did just fine, thanks, as did most of the kids. But it soon became apparent that this recital was not about the mastery of music. It was about doing something as well as you could, in front of your family and a room full of friendly strangers. It was a microcosm of life, and how to succeed in it: Do your best, be brief, then make room for the next guy. Share the limelight. Don't panic.

There was some bad violin. There always is. There was an unfortunate cello selection, Beethoven's "Minuet in G," the very piece that is mangled in "The Music Man." I kept wanting to point at my forehead and say, "Think! Think!" as the young girl valiantly struggled against the instrument. In the end, the girl won the match—she was unbowed. I wish I could say the same for the cello.

By rehearsal's end, I knew we'd all get through the recital in one piece. I let the rest of the family know about my guarded optimism. The next day was spent pretending that whatever was happening at 5:30 p.m. was no big deal. We left our house at 5:15. We walked across the street to the concert hall. (We live across the way from the college where our son takes piano lessons.) We probably could have just opened all our windows and let him play at home. But that wouldn't have been the same as surviving the recital. My husband brought along a camera with a flash attachment. He sat poised with the camera in front of his face the entire time our son played. He never took one picture until the very end. He caught the upside of our son's final bow. I knew why he didn't snap a shot. He was afraid the flash would startle our son out of his concentration and "Old MacDonald" would turn into "Kitten on the Keys", or "Mary Had a Little Lamb" into "Slaughter on 10th Avenue." Mayhem would ensue, tears would flow, and for what? A parental paparazzo? My husband made the right choice. After all, it's not like we'd need a Polaroid to refresh our memories. Before there were cameras, people just remembered stuff. It was a lot more economical that way, and required less storage space.

The rest of the recital was mostly short and mainly sweet. Some of the kids were quite good. One girl was quite bad, but gratefully she didn't know it. All of them were troupers who showed grace under pressure and sensitivity, too. You can't play or hear Beethoven, Bach, or Mozart—however rudimentary the execution or reception—without being humbled by the presence of such soul. And best of all, no one tripped, slipped, or skipped. A collective sigh of relief was breathed at the end of the afternoon.

God bless the parents for paying for the lessons, for showing up and listening, with the least of expectations, attentively to all. God bless the teachers for patiently instructing tiny fingers into finders of notes, chords, and (occasionally) music. And God bless the children for dressing neatly but not gaudily, for having good manners, and for playing, well, as well as can be expected. I'm hopeful that the musical path our son is on will eventually lead to our basement and long rehearsals with a high-school rock band. I don't want to push him, but I can dream, can't I?

Don't hurry, be Harriet

I was driving on the Hutchinson River Parkway the other day when I noticed that every car was passing me at a clip. I checked my speedometer. Sure enough, it was holding fast at 60, five miles over the posted speed limit. So I pulled back to 55. (It's always been my contention that the quicker the wit, the slower the driver.) Now even gravel trucks and school buses were leaving me in their dust. Where are all these people going, I wondered. And what in tarnation is the rush?

The rush, I suppose, is modern life. It whooshes all around us, and most of the time we whoosh right along with it. I know I do. But on this particular day I was in no particular hurry to be anywhere. I was just cruisin' while I was musin'. I was thinking about Harriet, the unhurried child. Harriet is six years old, and she never rushes. Harriet is the shared friend of my son and daughter.

Once while doing the rounds of after-school drop-offs (it was my turn to be car-pool commando), I asked Harriet if she wanted to walk with me. It's traditional in our town to hand-deliver, en masse, each child to his or her door. It makes an event out of going home. All the other kids had already bolted from the car, foiling the childproof door locks by climbing out the open windows. Not Harriet. She sat happily still in the back.

"No, that's ok," she replied, "I'll wait here and think. My mom lets me do that sometimes." After the dropped-off child had gone inside, the other kids shoved their way back into my car, where Harriet was happily lost in thought.

Oh, for a world full of Harriets. Not that my kids are always on fast-forward (there's bedtime, for example, and getting ready for school, otherwise known as "the snail's-pace circuit"). But more often than not they're in a rush, and sad to say, I'm often right behind them, pushing. Which is why I encourage their friendship with Harriet. She has an Old World sensibility. She has a grin like the Cheshire cat's, and she moves about as quickly as the "Who are you?" caterpillar of "Alice in Wonderland." She tends to slow things down somehow, even when the three of them are running pell-mell across the playground. They enjoy the run; they don't rush it.

I always feel when I'm in Harriet's presence that I'm going to learn something. More often than not, I do. I learn to linger in the present moment, not to move

8

so quickly to the next. I've never really understood the hubbub about being first, or learning fast. Walking at nine months, talking at one year, potty trained at 18 months, reading at 3. These days, the fast track starts at birth. No wonder we have so many harried, hurried drivers clogging the roadways. They've crammed too much into that sliver of time we call a day, and even though they were up at dawn, they're still running, late.

I hope that Harriet manages to maintain her inner stillness. It won't be easy, not the way things are going. Already the after-school activity options are spinning out of control. Ice-skating, piano lessons, horseback riding, soccer practice, ballet, karate, chess club, choir. Too much of too many good things. Are we having fun yet? I don't think so. Are we stressed out to the max? Very much so, thank you. And you?

Isn't it telling that the way we punish our children these days is to give them a "timeout"? Sounds more like a reward to me. We need a whole lot more time-outs, more non-Nintendo, off-line, unplugged moments of calm reflection. We need to slow down, and fast. Think of what all those speeding cars are doing to the highway infrastructure. Now think about what they're doing to the infra-structure of our selves. We need to start a movement, a slow one of course. We could call ourselves the Trail-Blazing Turtles. We're always on time, and we don't mind waiting. We've even been known to win a race or two. We like to take long walks. We don't hurry, we don't worry. We don't speed, we read. And yes, we already have our poster child: Harriet, the Spry.

My toddler is a Labrador Retriever

When I discovered my two-year-old daughter covered ear to chin with the new lipstick I'd just spent days and a tidy sum in the procurement thereof, believe me when I tell you I was not amused. Not one tiny bit.

At the time I was the full-time mother of not only one but two two-year-olds, plus a four-year-old. Intellectual stimulation was a thing of the past, any semblance of lasting order, you guessed it, a thing of the past. I was still a virtual newcomer to the wacky world of motherhood. (You think you know so much after four years in the trenches, but you don't even begin to be more than an absolute beginner until your child is 10. At least now I'm proud of my amateur standing.)

So there she stood grinning up at me, with my precious, new outrageously expensive lipstick not only covering her face, but also her hands, the sink, and the wallpaper in our rented house.

But you can't discipline a two-year-old the way you can an older child. Two-year-olds are basically the human version of a Labrador Retriever—full of energy and eager to please with zero comprehension of the English language. Sure they fake knowing what "no" means, but do they really? I don't think so.

So what's a mother to do? Yell, get upset, and make an even worse mess, emotionally as well as verbally? Been there, done that, seen it doesn't work. Not on a two-year-old. Not on an any-year-old. Who responds well to being yelled at? (I don't see anyone raising a hand—probably because you're afraid I'll slap it.)

Instead, I did the only thing I could do. I laughed. Then, I grabbed my camera, which for some reason is the one thing I can always find no matter how messy the house is, and took two pictures. One shows her beaming triumphantly, ever so pleased with her mess. The other photo, shot after I'd given her the classic "I'm not amused" stare shows her with an "uh-oh" look on her face. (You have to learn to cultivate your disapproving look. Sometimes it's your only line of defense.)

The passage of time has made me even more aware of how wrong it would have been to discipline her any further. The "whoops" in her eyes shows only that she's sad, not that she has any idea why.

After that we had a whopping good time cleaning her off, and cleaning the sink and the walls too. She said, "Sorry Mommy," in that earnest way that two-year-olds do, and I told her she couldn't wear lipstick again until she's 37.

But I was so glad then, and I'm even gladder now that I snapped a picture and didn't snap myself. Thank goodness for the saving grace of humor. It gives perspective on those trying little moments in life, that without a good laugh, or at least a sigh and a giggle can mushroom into anger and regret. Laughing at my children and myself has saved me on many occasions from saying and doing the wrong thing. Yes, of course, there's time for serious talk and correction, but I've found that most effective time-outs are the ones I enforce with a smile on my face. And no I don't always have a smile on my face. I'm a mother, remember?

But I also have photo proof when the chips are down I know how to take a joke. And a picture.

Skirting the issue of uniforms

There are many good reasons I could give for why I want my daughter to play field hockey. I could say that I want her to learn how to be a team player, to be well coordinated. Or that I think it's important for a 12-year-old girl to get physically tired, so tired that she won't argue about clearing the dishes off the table or finishing her homework, too tired even to IM her friends. (Like that's ever going to happen.)

Then there's Title IX. I love Title IX. I love having a daughter who benefits from Title IX. These are all perfectly valid and plausible causes. Unfortunately all of them are rational lies. Rational lies are what you tell when you're trying to rationalize.

The real reason I want my daughter to play field hockey is the skirt.

The blue plaid skirt that is the pièce de résistance of the girls' field-hockey uniform at my daughter's school. (As opposed to boys' field hockey, which I guess would be lacrosse.)

If she makes the team, she gets the skirt. I want the skirt. It's so much cuter, hipper, and cooler than any gym outfit or school uniform that I can remember. But I can't have it. It's not my school. It's not my time. So I have to be content to live through her. Just in this instance, I promise you.

I don't want to be a vicarious mom. I have my own life, thank you very much. (I know it's here somewhere. Perhaps under a pile of papers.) But I love my daughter, and I love this crazy sport: the click-clack crashing of the sticks, the running up and down the field, the white shirts, the plaid skirts.

It is almost too wonderful for words. But not quite.

I'm sure there was field hockey in southern California when I was growing up, but somehow it passed me by. I swam, I golfed, I volleyed, I arched, but I never got to be part of a sport that had a skirt requirement. I can't help feeling deprived because of this.

I keep asking my daughter to see if she can get an extra uniform in my size. She thinks I'm kidding, so she laughs and says, "Oh, Mom." If she knew the truth, she wouldn't think it was funny. She'd think it was totally weird. And she'd be right.

I had my shot at miniskirts, back when I was 12. And I have no problem wearing the "mother mini," which is more or less the length that Florence Henderson wore on "The Brady Bunch." That's what I've become: A brunette Carol Brady. (Does that mean I'm Carol Brunette?) I don't mind. But just once I wish I could whack my way across an autumn field, playing the game like all the other girls, with strength, stamina, camaraderie, and pizzazz.

No, actually, I don't. I just want to wear the skirt.

Life isn't supposed to be about fashion, but sometimes life is wardrobe. Sometimes what you wear defines who you are, if only in part, or for a time. I want my daughter to be what that skirt means to me. I want her to be hardworking, fun-loving, team-spirited, spunky, funky, running full out, a believer and an achiever.

And I want her to be all this in a really awesome outfit.

Is that too much for a mother to ask?

And if not her, then me. Or better yet, both of us. Her in her way, me in mine. Age-appropriate goals and clothing.

But why not, just this once, in matching field-hockey skirts?

Did Rockefeller start out like this?

What do you want to do this summer? we asked our children not long ago. Go to camp? Take swimming lessons? Lie on your back and make cloud animals in your mind? None of the above, our son and daughter answered. We want to make money.

They are 7. They are twins. They have enormous spending plans, plans that mainly involve candy, movies, and Beanie Babies far beyond their usual budget. They are tired of the dribs and drabs of pocket change we dole out. This summer they want to make the big bucks so they can spend it all. They want to feel the thrill of entrepreneurship.

They came up with what they hope will be a great notion: selling juice boxes at the beach. It seems a harmless enough plan, something that might even be met with appreciation from thirsty children whose mothers have forgotten (it happens) to pack refreshments. Our kids could be a kind of saving grace.

Our kids could clean up good.

The planning stages of the enterprise mainly involve my going to the supermarket and pricing the various varieties of apple versus grape juice. Apple wins out. It's cheaper, more thirst-quenching, and doesn't stain nearly as badly. (Personally, I'd rather drink paint remover than apple juice, but maybe I'm an anomaly.)

They will sell the juice boxes for 75 cents each, which is barely breaking even. We figure our kids are too young to fully appreciate the concept of a loss leader. Maybe next summer.

Day 1: Success is (a) relative

The first day out, they sell only one juice box. To their uncle, who is kind enough to give them a ride home from the beach, which is only two blocks from our house. So we don't feel too bad that our baby sitter has to walk home alone dragging the juice wagon behind her. At least our kids are learning proper managerial skills, such as delegating unpleasant tasks whenever possible. I only hope the baby sitter doesn't unionize.

Day 2: Right concept, wrong location?

Unfortunately, no relatives felicitously drive by today. Sales are nil. Maybe we're at the wrong beach. The throngs of children we were expecting seem to be elsewhere. Hmmm. Expectations and interest in the venture are beginning to flag. There is some talk of bigger and better signage, and an art project looms large in our future. But it is derailed, or at least postponed, by "Arthur." The kids have been out in the sun all day. A little public television never hurt anyone, did it?

Day 3: Gone fishing

No sales today either, but that's because the kids have gone fishing instead. Maybe a day away will give them some perspective. Maybe some success at, say, catching a fish will encourage them to persevere in their venture. No need to consider the project a complete failure yet. We still have 20 days on the beach-house rental, and the juice we don't sell here we can always hawk at home. And what isn't sold at home will provide me with several months' worth of school-lunch beverages.

The fishermen return empty-handed, though not glum. A tiger shark barely managed to get away, or so I'm told. And they've come up with a new idea, a different venue. There's a crafts fair tomorrow, and the kids want to set up their juice stand on the village green. I tell them OK, so long as their business is as far as possible from their aunt's. She is an artist of some note who sells her paintings at the fair every year. She is a kind, refined, and restrained woman who loves her niece and nephew dearly. I would hate to test the limits of her patience with the likes of our two darling yahoos screaming, "Juice for sale!" while she tries to make a living. We hope the locals will be both hungry for fine art and thirsty for fine beverages. We hope we don't spill any juice on her oil paintings.

Day 4: A fine day at the fair

The crafts fair our children intend to crash actually has a name and a brief but illustrious history. The arts festival has evolved (or rather devolved, depending upon how you view these things) into quite the event at this beach community.

It happens twice every summer: once in July and once in August. That way, whichever month you're here renting you get a crack at it. And the year-round folks have two opportunities to rake in a little extra cash. About a week before it takes place, handwritten signs announcing hours and sponsors spring up overnight at strategic places—the post office, along the main road into town. Even in high gear, it's fairly low-key: The fair lasts only four hours. It consists of a rolling balance of genuine artists and artisans, plus burgeoning capitalists like our own mop-tops selling everything from cookies to handmade beaded necklaces to shells filled with a small amount of wax and wick. (No one in her right mind would call it a candle, even if she did purchase one from a persistent six-year-old for a dollar when she couldn't haggle him down to 75 cents.)

We arrive at 10 a.m., fashionably late. It's a bright, sunny summer day and the village green is buzzing with activity. Incredibly, there is a space just the right size for our kids to set up their business right next to the library's used-books table. Tom Clancy for $1. (No, he can't be haggled down to 75 cents either.)

My husband and I wander away as quickly as possible, not wishing to hover. We say hello to my husband's sister but don't linger. She is right in the middle of about three transactions. Her paintings are really good. They are mostly beach and flower scenes, the type that forever remind one of this beautiful place. In a sense, she provides a way to take your vacation home. It's a cool way to make a living, I think.

But not as cool, of course, as selling juice boxes, which our children do with great aplomb, racking up a whopping $12 in an hour and a half.

Day 10: Business? What business?

It's been a week since the arts festival, and no one's said a thing about juice boxes. I have noticed, however, that someone keeps slipping them out of the refrigerator. The time is now taken up with morning summer camp, crabbing parties, and beach expeditions. Making money has lost its appeal.

Or rather, the grim reality of standing around in the summer sun with a cooler full of product has turned out to be less fun than they expected. Beachcombing is hot right now. So is watching the sunset and going on nature walks.

True, we spent a lot on the juice boxes, not to mention the summer rental, but it was for a good cause: to teach our children a well-worn truism. The best things in life are free. And the second-best things are on sale at a sizable markdown.

But that'll be next summer's lesson.

Either way, it's a welcome change

If I'd wanted to have summer all year round, I would have stayed in Los Angeles. I didn't. I wanted seasons, so I came East and, come to think of it, also North, where when it's really cold you can comfort yourself with the thought that soon it will be warmer. And vice versa.

Eventually, we all complain a little when the heat gets to be a bit too much, though usually sometime in late August I have a moment of weakness when I consider the possibility that wearing shorts and T-shirts all the time is perhaps a good thing. But the feeling always passes on the first crisp autumn day, when suddenly a sweater is required.

In the same way that I favor seasons, I'm also fond of summer vacation for kids. I don't think I'd do well on a year-round school calendar.

I think absence makes the heart grow fonder. I think kids need to miss going to school; that way, they want to go back. I look forward to the boredom that my children wrestle with, two-thirds of the way through their two months off. Boredom is the true mother of invention. (I should know. I'm a mother.)

By June I'm practically chomping at the bit, so very ready am I for school to be over, for the imposed structure of my children's schedule on my life to be lifted. I think we all need the lack of structure, whether we know it or not—a time to catch our breath and breathe deeply. If life is a merry-go-round, then there's no getting off. But at least in the summer, the horses start to saunter.

In our house, on our carousel, they do anyway. Work even shrinks a megabyte or two at my husband's office, allowing us all the occasional luxury of family dinners on weeknights, too. Last year, my kids didn't even go to day camp. We all read books, we all went swimming, we all hung out together as much as possible. For the first time, I didn't hire a baby sitter. (Why should I pay someone to ignore my children when I'll gladly do it for free?)

But by the first of September, I am almost giddy when I see those aisles and aisles of back-to-school displays at the supermarket and the stationery store. I would be a home-school disaster. I need to have my children do their learning somewhere else. I feel all my skills are taxed to the max just keeping them clothed and fed. And if you saw some of the meals I've cooked and some of the wardrobe choices I've made, you'd be glad my kids go to school, too.

Besides, by mid-July they've already heard all my jokes, which means seven weeks of summer repeats. When they're back in school, I can recharge, work on new material.

Also, by summer's end we're ready for some quality time—apart from each other. They find out who their teachers are, what classmates they'll have in the coming school year. They say they wish that summer would last forever, but we all know they don't really mean it. Endless summer would mean no trick-or-treating, no making cranberry sauce for Thanksgiving dinner, no Christmas caroling. Endless summer would be a bummer. I like things regulated. I like change. That's why I like the seasons and the school system.

So I want to thank state and local governments for providing my kids with a public-school education and for making education mandatory. Because on those rainy, dark December days when my kids start whining, "Why do we have to go to school?" I can simply hide my smile and best I can, and say without fear of contradiction, "because it's the law."

A brief field trip to my life after child-rearing

When my kids get back from their four-day school trip to Williamsburg, Virginia, I will ask them what they did, though I already know what they will answer: Nothing. No, really Mom. Nothing. It was sooooooo boring. And it rained. A lot. This is just what 12-year-olds say, initially anyway, when you inquire about their activities. It's not to be taken seriously.

Eventually they'll tell me most of what they did, and in the retelling they'll realize they had a pretty good time. They may have even learned something. But for now, my son will probably say the best part of the trip was watching "Ferris Bueller's Day Off" on the bus. My daughter has already called to complain about the hotel. She misses me, she misses her bed. Her shoes are wet. And she bought me a sock monkey. I'm not sure her social studies teacher will be pleased with her priorities. Maybe she should buy him a sock monkey too.

When my kids get back tomorrow from their four-day school trip to Williamsburg, Virginia, they will ask me what I did with all my free time. The time I usually spend driving them around or making them dinner or nagging them about their homework. They will assume I'll meet them at their bus with a finished novel and an exchange student from Finland, and that I'll be 10 pounds thinner. They have high expectations. They are also impatient. They like to see quick results. After all they've been away since Tuesday. Surely I've accomplished something.

The truth is, I haven't done much at all these last three days. I haven't gone into the city to see a play or an exhibit. I haven't written much. I haven't reorganized the closets. Nor have I taken up race-car driving or gambling or started playing bridge. What I have done is some thinking, about what life will be like six years from now.

Six years from now my kids will be in college, I hope. And since they are twins and it's unlikely one will be held back or skip a grade, it's safe to assume they'll be leaving the nest simultaneously.

When I think back to the first six years of their lives, it seems like a slow march through molasses just getting them to first grade. The second six years, however, have been more like a quick step danced to an increasingly faster tempo. I fear the next six years will blur right past and then—all at once—they'll be gone. Not gone for good, but gone in a way they've never been gone before. Gone as in "going on with their lives." It's the goal of having kids: If you succeed, they grow up and go away.

Perhaps I'm suffering from fear of success. I'm used to having my children structure my day, my thoughts, my breathing. Little by little, they aren't that structure any more. What I'm left with is me.

I remember me: I used to spend a lot of time with me, before I was married. And even after marriage I had a daytime gig living a solo life. But motherhood changed that in ways I never could have imagined. My thoughts are no longer my own. They belong to two other people who you could say are renting space in my head. You could also call them squatters: They came in and took over. When they don't live here anymore I don't think they'll be as demanding. (But I wouldn't be surprised if they FedExed their dirty laundry home…just to give me a head start. They're thoughtful in their way.) And so it seems prudent to plan for the six years that will follow the next six. I'll read, I'll write, maybe I'll travel…into the city for lunch with my husband. I'll have a grand old time I'm sure. I'll find my bearings eventually without them. I'll have to, so I will.

But the best-laid plans of mice and men and me can be quite cheesy. So I'm not trying to plan as much as I'm trying to unlock the grip my children have on my heart. So that maybe it can beat on its own when the time comes for them to go.

And yet I also know that when my kids come back tomorrow from their four-day school trip to Williamsburg, Virginia, the only thing I'll want to hear is not what they did or what they saw or what they learned. The only thing I'll want to hear is their hearts beating close to mine when I hold them in my arms.

Pets

Not a whale of a tale,
but definitely fishy

About three years ago, Anna and her family—one husband and four kids ranging in age from 9 years to 6 months—went to Wyoming for a week-long summer vacation. They took along their baby sitter, too, a lovely and loyal young woman from the Philippines whose name is Tien Sing.

The week went by quickly. They all had fun riding horses and doing Western stuff. The last day of vacation they went to a fair. The 9-year-old, Carolyn, got to wrestle a pig (a high point of any vacation) and throw Ping-Pong balls at a target. These were separate events. Carolyn threw the balls so well that she was given a prize—a goldfish in a water-filled plastic bag.

After the initial feeling of pride at her accomplishment, Carolyn (ever the sensible child) thought it would be best to leave the fish in Wyoming, either by giving it to a local child or setting it free in a stream.

"Fair fish never last," Carolyn told me later; that was her reasoning at the time. Tien Sing would have none of it. In her eyes, the fish was now part of the family and should be treated as such. Tien Sing carefully transferred the fish from plastic bag to glass jar, one that had previously contained baby food. She even poked holes in the jar lid, to make sure the fish could get enough air. Anna and Tom were so focused on getting the family home that they let Tien Sing have her way. And her fish.

Then they left for the airport. They had to change planes in Salt Lake City, but their first flight was delayed. When they got to Salt Lake, their plane was still on the runway, but all but one of their tickets had been reassigned to other passengers on the overbooked flight.

Tom could have done the selfish, if understandable thing, and flown home alone. He had to be at work the next morning. But Tom is not the sort of man who abandons his wife and four children (and don't forget the fish), so the plane flew off without him.

The airline offered to fly them all to Phoenix, but since they live in New York, this didn't make a whole lot of sense. In fact, the suggestion was a tad irksome—especially when Anna heard a boarding announcement for a flight to Boston, which most would agree is closer to New York than Arizona is.

They got on the flight to Boston. Tien Sing clung to the fish in the jar, monitoring its every move. They arrived at Logan Airport a little after 1 in the morning. They were all a little groggy by then. And Tien Sing was distracted by her real job, which was to help keep an eye on the four sleepy, cranky children. Twice the fish was left behind, once at a newspaper kiosk in the airport, once at the car rental desk. Both times the family was called back to reclaim their prize. They just couldn't seem to shake that fish.

They drove from Boston to New York in a car that was way too small for them. They were packed in like sardines. Fortunately—and I use this word ironically—their luggage had been lost, so they didn't have to pile all their bags on top of themselves. (The bags did show up, but about a week later.)

Somewhere on Interstate 95 going south, Tien Sing gasped in horror. She had not kept her eye on the ball (or, rather, fish), and the water in the baby-food jar had spilled. The little rascal was gasping for…water. It had some but not enough, not nearly enough to make the journey home. About a quarter-inch's worth. Quick-thinking Anna grabbed her bottle of Evian and poured it over the fish, who settled down immediately and started swimming around again, fit as a fan tail. Only now the fish was undoubtedly a poisson. And feeling very chichi, if a trifle fatigué.

The family arrived at their suburban home by 5 a.m. Tom slept for 90 minutes, then got up and went to work in downtown Manhattan. Mission accomplished. Family home safe.

And the fish? The fair fish that should not have lasted? Three years later, it's still going strong. But they still haven't named it. They just call it "fish." But then what's in a name? A fish by any other name would smell, well, you know. Fishy.

How we got a dog
we already had

There's a famous old saying I just made up that goes, "into every life, a little dog must fall." And Charlie is the dog that fell into our lives. It was inevitable, I suppose. First comes love, then comes marriage, then children, then a house with a small backyard. It all points inexorably toward one goal: the acquisition of a pet. Granted, I stalled for as long as I possibly could, using all the standard excuses: new carpets; too much responsibility for small children; what if we go on vacation. But eventually the kids and the carpets got older, and we never go on vacation anyway. When our youngest daughter started capturing caterpillars and giving them names like Wendell and Fuzzy, well, I knew the jig was up.

So like any self-respecting, cautious couple, my husband and I did research, which meant standing in one of those mega-bookstores for half an hour, leafing through the "pets" section. I found a paperback called "Finding the Right Dog for You" and skipped to the part about the best breeds for young children, cross-referencing with dogs that don't shed. I came up with a small and unattractive list of dogs. I won't mention any names. Some of you may already own these dogs, even love them. I didn't. But then I saw the name of a dog I'd never heard of before: a Border Terrier. Well sure, I knew from terriers, but the "border" business caught my eye. So did the picture. This dog looked as though he belonged in the section titled "Mutts and Mixed Breeds." I read on. Turns out the Border Terrier is the 67th most popular dog in the country. I liked this fact. Turns out they're great with kids, don't shed, and are very smart.

So we bought a book on terriers, contacted the American Kennel Association, found out how to reach the Border Terrier Association, and received a nationwide list of accredited Border Terrier breeders. We said nothing to the kids. Having made the decision to call only those within driving distance of us—although I've heard of cases where people actually have their pets flown in from the far reaches of the globe (go figure)—my list of possible breeders was short. The first two had no dogs available. The third one was in Connecticut, one state away, but only an hour's drive, so I allowed for the possibility of crossing state lines for a pet purchase. After all, many people drive from Connecticut to New York and back on a daily basis. But that's another essay.

The woman who answers the phone says she has two dogs available, a nine-month-old girl named Daisy and a two-year-old boy named Charlie. The word "puppy" is never mentioned, which is good because the last thing I want is a puppy. She also proceeds to grill me, politely, about why I want this particular breed. Actually, she asks the questions and then answers them. She says: "You probably want a Border Terrier because you've read they're good with kids, don't shed, and are very smart." I wonder if she was reading over my shoulder at the bookstore. I ask her if I'm mistaken in my assumptions. She says no, I'm not, but I can tell she is a fierce defender of the breed and is not going to give up one of her dogs to just any old happy-go-lucky family. We are going to have to prove ourselves worthy. We set up a time for us to drive to her house to see the dogs. It's in a rural area. I'm expecting a dirt road, chicken-wire fencing, and a nice but messy lady in a small house overrun with dogs. I am so wrong.

What we find is a beautiful country road leading to a white Colonial house surrounded by green rolling pastures and a woman I suspect is the real Martha Stewart. Except that she says her name is Carlie. Her home and her dogs are immaculate. She has hot pizza waiting for us in the kitchen. Even her husband, just returned from an eight-mile run, is tidier than I'll ever be. I wonder if owning a Border Terrier will bring out all this harmony and order in my own life. Now I really want a dog.

But the Border Terrier named Daisy and I don't hit it off. Nothing personal; she's cute, sort of, but has all the personality of sweater pilling. I'm a tougher sell than even I suspected. After all, we all know who's going to be walking and feeding and spending the most time with this canine child. Not the father with the impossibly long hours at work. Not the kids with the incredibly short attention spans. Who does that leave? All together now, ladies. The mom.

And then Charlie comes into the room. First he does this cute little I'm-a-fun-dog dance for the kids. Then he licks my husband's hand. Then he jumps into my lap and settles in for a long nap. It's like he's already our dog. We just hadn't noticed until now.

We don't take him home with us. We all decide to think about it. I hem and haw about keeping him off the road and on our property. We find a workable solution, and suddenly our home seems lacking in some way. It's not that we need a dog. It's just that we need Charlie.

Three weeks later, Carlie delivers Charlie to our door. She is glad he's found a good family to adopt him, and I am flattered that she holds us in such high esteem. Because I know she is sorry to see him go. I realize I've gotten more than a new dog; I also have a new friend. Charlie's aunt, so to speak. And she likes my kids, so I can tell our friendship will grow in whatever space becomes available between two active lives lived 40 miles apart.

Charlie acts as if he's back after a brief vacation. He curls up on his favorite couch, the one he's never seen before, and encourages us all to pet him. There is no settling-in period. I guess we've always had a dog.

Happily at the end of our leash

Charlie was a show dog once; never made the major leagues, but to borrow from the movie "On the Waterfront," he could have been a contender. Rosie never was.

Well, there was one brief foray, a rather small-time kennel-club beauty pageant in which Rosie was awarded...nothing. Not even Miss Congeniality.

Rosie is one of those canines coquettishly referred to as "pet quality." It's the animal-world equivalent of having a good personality.

Rosie is no rose. Charlie has the looks. Rosie is steadfast and loving and true. Everything that a pet needs to be. Not a looker, but a keeper, to be sure.

Both of them are Border Terriers, a slightly unusual and possibly unpopular breed of dog, depending upon your point of view. They love people, all people, family members and strangers alike. They love children—good ones and tail pullers. They wouldn't harm a hair of a homo sapiens's head.

But dogs are an entirely different matter. When it comes to dogs, they love each other. And that's about it.

We truly adore them and wouldn't trade our two tenacious terriers for anything in the world—not money or fame, not even a loveable Lab. They are ours forever, but we wouldn't advise getting one for your very own.

Unless you're incredibly fond of barking, and you never want to stop to talk to a neighbor while walking your dog. Oh, you can talk to the neighbors without pets all you want. But they're rarely out walking (they're usually jogging, so not in the mood for chit chat). The ones out walking usually have dogs at the end of a leash, like we do.

My husband and I love walking our dogs, in theory at least. We love the extra bit of exercise it affords us, the chance to talk, to see the neighborhood, to see the neighbors. But most of our neighbors, like us, have dogs.

Friendly dogs, dogs that want to sniff and pant and say "How's it going, Charlie? How ya doin', Rose? Ow!!! Whadja try and bite me for? I was only sayin' hello!!"

Cheeks tinged with red, we make loud disciplining noises, offer our sincere and heartfelt apologies, and make sure no real damage has been done. And then we beat a hasty retreat, pulling our miscreant hounds behind us, vowing, once again, never to stop and say hello, or even smell the roses, unless no one else is anywhere in sight.

Gratefully, our neighbors are a most forgiving group. The ones who know us best just smile and keep on walking, picking up the pace a bit, just as we do. We sigh, we shake our heads and say, "Next time, Labradors."

But would Labs be any better, or is this just a dog-fancier's pipe dream—the hope of a breed that would accommodate an occasional brief conversation with other pet owners? These animals do exist; I've seen them. Surely it isn't us, the innocent owners, who bring out this sort of anti-social behavior in our dogs? We've given them every opportunity: a nice town, quiet, tree-lined streets. What more could they want? To rule the world, is my guess. One retriever at a time.

Other terrier owners understand us all too well. The Westies, Scotties, and Jack Russells we sometimes run into—and then run away from—are just as raucous and rude as our two little pedigreed mutts. Their owners looks every bit as chagrined as we do, as they scurry past us, holding onto the leash for dear life. So we've come to the conclusion that it's not just our subset, it's the terrier world. Maybe they should just call them terrors instead.

And yet everyone who ever sees our dogs always tells us how cute they are, how good looking. Well, they always say that Charlie is handsome. Then they say, "And Rosie's such a sweet dog, isn't she?" And she is, come to think of it (when she's not chasing rabbits or yapping at a passing poodle). And isn't that more important than possessing fleeting good looks? Shouldn't sweetness count for something? Maybe not in the rarified dog-show world, but in our house it matters a lot.

I'm sure it matters to Charlie, too, if I may be so bold (foolish?) as to second-guess a dog. He's loyal and true. But he's also a looker. We love him just the same, though every now and then we sense he feels a little superior to the rest of us.

Maybe after being judged so often in his former life (the two years before we got him), after winning so many blue ribbons, he knows how to spot a champion. And he also knows pet quality when he sees it.

I'd like to think he's judged us best-in-show when it comes to owners. But the way he sometimes looks, first at me and then at Rosie—well, let's just say I have my doubts.

Way-too-close encounters of the furred kind

The thing about surreal suburbia, land of neat lawns and sedate sidewalks, is the occasional touch of rural reality. We can't ever quite forget we inhabit a planet—a co-op, really—filled with all sorts of creatures. On the quarter-acre we call home, we have squirrels, raccoons, cardinals, and skunks. The skunks were never a problem, other than the occasional whiff of skunk aroma hanging in the summer air. But then we got a dog. And then the dog got skunked.

I'm not sure how it happened; I don't know who surprised whom. I only know I was saying good night to my daughter when our noses told us something was terribly wrong outside her open window. Skunk! was my first thought. (Actually, it was "monster skunk!" We were on the second floor, you see.) This was quickly followed by my next thought—Charlie!

Our dogged dog had just been let out for his evening run around the house. The timing was bad, but my hope was that somehow, some way, Charlie had been where the skunk hadn't.

But when Charlie came back inside it was immediately apparent that he and the skunk had occupied the same space at the wrong time. Charlie was clearly the loser. He looked chagrined.

The family leaped into action. Tomato juice, someone said, I think it was my son. My husband bravely held his breath and lifted Charlie into the tub, trying to remove some of the skunkiness with mere soap and water. But we didn't have any tomato juice. We had plenty of orange juice, but we figured that would only make him sticky and probably attract bees. So we improvised. We slathered him with spaghetti sauce, the kind that has large chunks of onion and garlic. Charlie smelled like a skunk who'd eaten a great Italian meal. He managed to maintain his dogly dignity, but only barely.

The next day we tried vinegar, another recommended remedy. That made Charlie smell like a skunk dying Easter eggs. Charlie was cooperative, but clearly not pleased. The day after that I bought tomato juice, and we gave Charlie an out-of-doors tomato-juice rubdown and rinse. My son said Charlie smelled like a skunk eating tomatoes.

I wish there were such a fruit or vegetable as a skunk-eating tomato. I'd plant them in my garden and let them eat the skunks. Unfortunately, no such plant exists. And besides, I don't have a garden. I don't have the patience of a gardener. I have the patience of a shopper. I was willing to buy any product that promised olfactory relief. I was willing to try anything. That's why Charlie was so nervous.

It soon became apparent that nothing really worked, except for the passage of time. We sudsed-up Charlie in dog shampoo: It made his skunky fur shiny and tangle-free. Charlie maintained an attitude of stoic endurance, but he was beginning to show signs of strain. The sight of a shopping bag or a garden hose made him flinch.

Two weeks later we almost had our dog back to his original scent. Then—bingo! Charlie and the skunk collided again. Or maybe it was a different skunk this time. (I never see them, I only smell them.) The score was now: Skunks 2, Border Terrier zip. And the whole horrendously humiliating and mostly ineffective washing process started all over again.

Charlie took to skulking in and out of rooms, looking sheepish and smelling skunkish. Our once-effusive terrier had turned into pariah puppy. We tried to assure him we still loved him, even as we tried to reassure ourselves he wouldn't always smell this bad. We started making him sleep in the basement. Charlie took this abasement badly. He was now skulking and slinking. He was practically lurking. We bought products with names like Skunk-Away and Skunk No More, and sprayed them lavishly on his fur, like they were French perfume. This only made him more despondent. He knew there was something wrong, only he couldn't quite put his paw on it. We hope he never does. We're just not up for skunking No. 3. Not yet.

Finally, we realized the trick is not tomato juice or vinegar or shampoo, or peroxide (which will turn your odorous dog a lovely shade of blond), or any other product for that matter. The trick, as G. Gordon Liddy so aptly put it when explaining how he could hold his hand over an open flame, is not minding. It's been almost a month now since the last close encounter of a skunk kind. You could say Charlie's his old self again. Or you could say we've learned not to mind.

We have a friend whose Jack Russell terrier once had 15 run-ins with a skunk, and this not in a lifetime, either. Just one bad summer. We're hoping Charlie doesn't beat his record. Otherwise, we might have to get Charlie a copy of "How to Be Your Own Best Friend."

Charlie craves a little more respect

My dog doesn't have a demanding job. He isn't expected to fetch, sit, or roll over. I don't ask him to do the laundry, drive the kids to school, or hold up his end of the dinner conversation. I only want him to do one thing, and that is to come when I call him. And for some reason, lately he's developed a wait-and-see attitude about his one and only task.

He usually comes when it's dinner time, though he's gotten rather picky about the dog food we've been feeding him. And he always comes when it's time to go for a walk. But bedtime is another story.

Charlie sleeps in the basement. Charlie doesn't like this. Charlie feels his rightful bed is on the second floor with the rest of the family. He'll gladly sleep in any one of our beds—he's not choosy. He just wants to get off the floor. And out of the basement.

So when I put him out at night for his last chance to sniff the evening air and bark at passersby, I wait a suitable interval and then call him. I call softly at first so as not to disturb the neighbors, then gradually louder until I sometimes reach a drill-sergeant's pitch.

Usually I find Charlie sitting some seven feet away from me, head slung low in the darkness, refusing to budge until I move toward him. Then he scurries in, but tries to dodge my attempts to shoo him down to the basement. The very nice basement, I might add, with the soft dog bed and doggie treats awaiting him. The very basement that my other dog, Rosie, has no trouble sleeping in.

Charlie's nighttime ritual also includes refusing to eat the bedtime snacks I offer on my upturned palm, then leave on the ground in front of him. Until I turn away, that is. He wants to make the point that he's not happy with me and he can't be bought. But he doesn't want Rosie getting the extra biscuits, so he always manages to snarfle them down.

Charlie is mostly a happy chap but he's always had a stubborn side. He's a terrier, you see. He will run after a ball if I throw it; he'll even bring it back to me. But he'll never let me have it back. He grips it in his teeth and plays tug-o'-war with it and me. He's mostly calm, but occasionally demanding. If he wants to be patted, he'll position his head right under my hand and move back and forth, as if showing me how the job should be done—by a trained professional, like him.

I love him dearly, but I have my stubborn side, too. I will walk him, feed him, pat him, and even let him nap on the good rug. But I won't let him sleep upstairs at night.

Why? Because he barks at every passing squirrel, car, dog, and jogger. He barks loudly and sporadically. He sits by the picture window in our living room, standing guard and waiting to sound the alarm. Over and over again. This is, dare I say it, unpleasant during daytime hours. But it's a bona fide deal-breaker at night. It's hard to sleep through or around his barking. In the basement, he is without benefit of a window, so he gives up and goes to doggie slumber land.

Worst of all, Charlie feels he should sleep not only on our bed, but in it, with his head preferably on my pillow. With his dog breath in my face all night.

I don't think so.

So in the basement Charlie sleeps, and my punishment for this is that Charlie won't come when I call him. Call it a stalemate between soul mates, my dog Charlie and I.

I think the main difference between our two dogs is that Rosie knows she's a canine pet, but Charlie thinks he's a person; a member of the family who should be treated with respect—and not just with dog treats. Charlie doesn't mind having a dog. He just doesn't want to sleep with one.

I understand completely.

A dog's a dog for a' that

A few years ago our dog Charlie lost an eye. At the risk of sounding brusque, that's what happened. I don't mean to make him sound careless either. He obviously didn't misplace it—it occurred because of a nocturnal run in with some unidentified animal, possibly wild. We suspect a raccoon, but it could have been a neighbor's cat. We don't blame any of the animals involved, certainly not Charlie. He's a dog, he got into a fight. Dogs do that on occasion. For all we know he may have won the fight. If Charlie could speak he'd probably say you shoulda seen the other guy.

It didn't happen overnight, the loss of his eye that is. Like most bad things it was a gradual loss, starting with a simple scratch. Our kindly vet—the kind of man dogs literally jump into the arms of—did every thing he could to save Charlie's eye, but after months of treatment it was clear that he'd gone blind in that eye and that it was causing him pain. Probably a great deal of pain, but Charlie's a terrier, hence stoic by nature, so he bore his discomfort with canine grace. But we couldn't bear the idea of him suffering. And so the eye had to go. Our vet strongly advised us against giving Charlie a fake eye. Apparently some pet owners do that, but for the life of me, I can't imagine why. Charlie's a dog, not a person. He doesn't have to worry about appearances. We were worried of course, about how he'd feel and how he would adapt. But what we've learned in the years that have followed is that losing an eye, for a dog anyway, sounds a lot worse than it is.

For one thing, as I mentioned before, Charlie's a terrier, and terriers are a tough little breed. They can deal with just about anything. They're sturdy, hardy and spunky. They don't whine or complain and they hate to be coddled. Charlie runs just as fast, sees spilt food just as quickly and leaps up for a pat on the head just as high as he always did. Clearly he's learned to make do and do well.

He even looks a bit more distinguished now, almost rakish. He appears to be winking at all times, giving him a jaunty, man about town look. I don't mean to make fun of Charlie's misfortune. It's something I obviously wish had never happened. But sometimes bad things happen, despite our best efforts, or when we're caught off guard. And Charlie has taught me an important lesson through all this. To be dogged if you will in the face of adversity, just like Charlie has been. He

34

has a wonderful life with us, and he seems to know it too. He's loved, fed, walked, and petted by at least four people a day. And he can see and hear and smell and feel the warm breeze on his face in the summer, the icy whoosh of wind in the winter. He prefers the summer. He's not that dogged. He seems to be grateful for all of that too. He's a dog to be proud of, and we are. Most of the time that is.

Because the thing of it is, Charlie is still just Charlie. Nothing seems to change him. For better or for worse. There are some things I wish I could change, but I can't, and believe me I've tried, so I've learned to accept them. Like the fact that he just doesn't like other dogs, except for his own dog, our other dog Rosie. The fact that he'll knock over any and all garbage cans whenever he gets the opportunity. The fact that he'll always lick me. Yuck.

Most things about him though I wouldn't change for all the world. Those are the things I've come to appreciate even more since he lost his eye. The way he likes to sleep outside my son's door when my son is at school, like he's been hired as a security guard. A somnolent security guard. The way he leaps several feet in the air every time my husband comes home, like he's been reunited with his long lost best chum, the one he hasn't seen since….this morning. The fact that he is simply and inexorably Charlie.

There is a lovely Shaker hymn called "Simple Gifts." For me it sums up what is best about dogs and other unaffected creatures, who are occasionally human. The song begins, "Tis the gift to be simple," and I quite agree. Because it truly is a gift to be uncomplicated, without angst. I think that's why we people love our pets, love animals of all kinds. They seem to live in utter simplicity, without duplicity. Or maybe it's the fact that they can't speak, so they can't complain. OK, occasionally they whine. But they've also been known to purr. And sing. And even bark for joy.

Modern life tries so hard to make us complex and obtuse. Simple is so much better. Just ask Charlie. If he could talk, I guarantee he'd tell you, it's true.

She walks the walk; will she talk the talk?

Our cockatiel can't talk, or maybe she just won't. She sings beautifully—like a bird, actually. She also hisses when she's feeling peevish, and once I swore I heard her hoot. But she hasn't said a word since we got her a year ago.

We used to think it was because she was so young, and that given time she'd step up to the plate, phonetically speaking. But we can't cover for her anymore. Clearly, she's just not a talker. In fact, she stubbornly refuses to engage in conversation.

For the last 12 months, I've stood in front of her cage every morning and said "Hello!" until I'm too embarrassed to go on. My embarrassment stems from the look of concern Tweety always gives me, as if she's thinking, "What are you, some kind of nut?" At this point I think it's far more likely that our dog will have the last word, and the first one, too. At least he always looks as if he's about to say something.

Part of the problem is that I've always been a skeptic when it comes to conversing with the animal kingdom. I'd be more than happy to hold forth with the celluloid Tweety Bird of Warner Bros. fame. But a real one? I'm just not sure. For me, this falls into the same category as clothing on animals: cats in bonnets, dogs in sweaters, cows in hats. It's just not natural, unless you like that sort of thing.

Which brings me to my sister-in-law. She's like a combination Anne of Green Gables and Dr. Doolittle. She talks to the animals, all right, and they talk back. She has an Australian parrot named Tuppy who's a regular fountain of information, a chatterbox with wings. She also has three dogs, a Vietnamese pot-bellied pig, a donkey, three goats, an occasional cow, and a rabbit. I bet they all talk, too, but she's too modest to admit it.

She lives on a farm (you probably figured that out on your own) with her husband and daughter. She's good with all living creatures, including people. But lately I've been dodging her calls because I'm embarrassed by our dumbfounded bird.

I just know I'll get an earful of Tuppy's latest bon mots, and then there'll be silence on the line while my sister-in-law waits for me to jump in with what Tweety's been up to. The pause will grow cavernous, and finally my sister-in-law will chirp, "Any success getting Tweety to talk yet?" And I'll squawk back, "Not a peep!"

It's not as if I haven't given it my best shot. I even broke down and bought a cassette tape called "Teaching Your Cockatiel to Talk." I had it for a month before I played it. I was too embarrassed. I didn't want to admit that our bird needed tutoring.

Finally, I set up the tape recorder and played the cassette for Tweety. Side 1 consisted of a man whistling "Yankee Doodle" about 50 times, followed by "Pop Goes the Weasel" 142 times (or so it seemed), followed by "Shave and a Haircut (Two Bits)" so many times that my eyes began to water and my son ran into the room, eyes bugging out, screaming, "Turn that thing off!"

Tweety, meanwhile, said nothing, although she did look slightly annoyed. I half expected her to pull out her own cassette tape, "How to Teach Your Humans to Mind Their Own Business."

The next day, my husband played Side 2 for Tweety. Side 2 was even worse than Side 1. It consisted of a woman saying phrases in an increasingly testy tone of voice, as if somehow she knew the bird wasn't getting it. "I love you, I love you, I love you," said in a maniacally singsongy tone, oh, 400 times, will make just about anyone feel cranky.

Then the voice on the tape started asking, "Do you want to play with me?" "No!" I kept answering, in an ever-louder bark.

Our dog was now convinced he'd done or was about to do something terribly wrong. The tape would say, "Do you want to play with me?" I'd shout back "No!" and Charlie would put his tail between his legs and beg to be let outside.

This went on for several minutes. Tweety didn't say a word, but she flapped her wings impatiently. And for the rest of the day we found ourselves saying, "I love you; do you want to play with me?" to each other: my husband to my son, my son to his sister. We all learned to say lots of silly things. And how to whistle, too.

I think Tweety is pleased with our progress, but I can only guess. She's still not talking.

Mothers and others

What I was doing
on Mother's Day

How I ended up spending Mother's Day at Yankee Stadium, I'll never know. Well, that's not exactly true. I was the one who bought the tickets weeks ago, fully aware of what day it was.

Partly it was the fact that Yankee management, in its infinite wisdom, had designated May 9 as Beanie Baby Day. Although we are now four years into the Beanie Baby craze, my kids show no sign of losing interest. Partly it was the synchronicity of the two events—baseball and Mother's Day (and don't forget the Beanie Babies). I am the daughter of a man who once gave his mother a baseball mitt for Mother's Day, a man who had season tickets to the Los Angeles Dodgers for most of the 1960s. I am the girl who wore a Dodgers' No. 8, John Roseboro uniform to every Dodger game I attended, at least until I outgrew it. I am both my father's daughter and my children's mother. But most of all I am a lover of baseball games.

I am not athletic by any stretch of the most benevolent imagination. But I love the ballet of baseball, the way the game works. It's so pastoral, so theatrical: It's a lot like life. Not much happens, and then all at once—wow!—there's a line drive, a boggled ball, a stolen base, a tag at the plate. Intensity in high relief to the dreamlike state the game pretends to be.

But through it all is this pulse of attention and focus that locks teammates together, even though they seem randomly scattered across a field. Which makes a baseball team more than a little bit like a family. They seem disconnected until they're called upon to pull together. Sometimes they do, and sometimes they don't. When it works, it's a beautiful thing to behold. When it doesn't, you want to look the other way. As I said, just like families.

I love the baseball uniforms, the way they seem like business suits for clowns. I love the seventh-inning stretch, the singing of "Take Me Out to the Ball Game," which was supplanted on Mother's Day by the singing of "Let Me Call You Sweetheart."

41

This was a very bad idea. For one thing, who the heck knows the words to "Let Me Call You Sweetheart"? Yes, I do happen to know them, but I am cursed with a jukebox for a brain.

The rest of the fans swayed nervously to the music and tried to mumble along. The other mothers shook their heads in disbelief. We came to sing, they seemed to say, not to be serenaded. We were a crackerjack bunch of mothers out there in the Bronx. We weren't throwing our day away for peanuts. We weren't a bunch of hot dogs. We were doing that thing that mothers do best: being there for others. And having a good time ourselves.

There is a sci-fi view of Mother's Day, seen mostly on TV, of women I call "adulation moms." In this conspicuous-consumption scenario, we mothers are off at a Sunday brunch with the nervous-necktie crowd, insisting on endless orange-juice toasts in our honor. Or sometimes we're portrayed as "it's about me" moms, drumming our lacquered nails impatiently, looking for the next present to unwrap and it had better not be some handmade card or art-class pottery monstrosity.

Those moms don't exist. They belong to the infantile imagination of an ad campaign. They were not attending Beanie Baby Day at Yankee Stadium, and it's a good thing. We baseball moms would have thrown them out for giving the rest of us a bad name.

Women like me who were idiotic enough to spend Mother's Day with 49,000 people on a gorgeous May day with the Yankees winning, 6-1, knew they were the real winners. We were with our families, the people who made us mothers, and life was glorious. That, the free Beanie Babies, and, as I said before, the Yankees winning, 6-1.

But the best part of the game (and my kids agree with me on this, although I'm pretty sure my husband doesn't), was not Derek Jeter's two-run homer, as beautiful as that was. It was the grounds crew. They dragged the field before the start of the sixth inning to the tune of "YMCA," by the Village People, and danced in time to the music as they did their otherwise boring but important job. That made me think of mothers again, doing boring but important jobs. We're the family field sweepers, but there's no law that says we can't do a little dance while we're at it.

And that's what Mother's Day at Yankee stadium meant to me. It was my little dance.

Mom's night write

I don't like writing at night any more. It used to be my favorite time of day to work. When the world was quiet, when thoughts were still, the words would flow and occasionally they'd make sense. In the morning, I could edit and then pass off the results as an article. That was B.C.: Before Children. Now I'm good if I'm able to stay up past 10, and then it's only because I'm waiting for my husband. (His hours are even worse than mine.)

But in the summertime, when the sun stays in the sky a few hours longer and the kids have nothing pressing to be up for in the morning, I can relax a little. I can stay up past my bedtime. And when the kids are finally asleep, sometimes I can focus my bleary eyes on the blue screen of my word processor and my tired little fingers can actually type a few words. What these moments lack in clarity, they more than make up for in quietness. Working at night somehow implies a deadline. I no longer have one. I write when I can. A woman can write whenever she wants to, but a mother had better wedge her bursts of creativity into the hours when her children are either at school or asleep

But of all the dual careers, writer/mom is probably the best. It certainly makes the Top 5 list, along with, say, painter/mom (although the kids would always want to help out). And how about pet-store-owner/mom? Of course the kids would always want you to bring your work home. The drawback of being a writer/mom: Writing takes a long time. So does raising children. The advantage: Writing takes a long time. So does raising children. As long as you're not in a hurry to finish either job, you'll do just fine.

Writing does not require an extensive wardrobe; neither does child-rearing. The money you save on clothes can be plowed into other priority items: paper, pens, ice cream. Writing requires a flexible schedule—ditto the mom thing. Your kids will have the most inflexible schedule this side of the diplomatic corps. There will be school, after-school activities, play dates, birthday parties. You will have to work around them. You will not be allowed to whine about this. It's part of the job. You knew that when you took it. Well, you sort of knew—your mother tried to warn you. You didn't listen. You were so sure you'd be different. Now you're not only starting to sound like your mom, you're beginning to dress like her, too. Hey, sweater sets can be cool. I think.

Your mom even suggested you try writing at night when the kids are asleep. You were only half-listening because the kids were making so much noise, so you thought she told you to buy a night light. You couldn't figure out why—you can't really write by it. But at least the light isn't so bright it wakes up the kids. Then it hits you like a duh-o-gram: The computer screen is the night light for the night write. And suddenly you feel very, very cozy. And as you doze off face first on your keyboard, you try very hard to have your nose hit the "save" key and not "delete."

Mr. Mom, in a whirl of his own

It's not like Mac meant to shame us; it's just that we were so messy by comparison. "How can anyone be so tidy in a room full of toddlers?" we'd wonder (shamefully). But the real problem was that we didn't know how to relate to Mac. (It might have helped if he'd been more unkempt.) He clearly wasn't "one of the girls."

I first met Mac at the local library's story hour, when my kids were still too young to read, but old enough to sit still—at least for a very short while. Mac is a stay-at-home dad in a town full of nannies and two-income families. Even in this loosey-goosey new millennium, Mac is, to say the least, a rare bird.

Mac was an actor before he had kids, but now he mostly spends his time as primary caregiver (otherwise known as benevolent schlepper), a role usually relegated to us, the stay-at-home moms. He takes his son and daughter to school, he picks them up, he does the shopping; in other words, he does the stuff that mothers usually do.

And to make matters worse, he's not a wuss or a groovy guy. He's just a guy. Which means he's not at all like us full-time moms. We are the strong, the proud, the few, and yes, the female. Mac is stronger, prouder, fewer, and did I mention Mac's a man? So at library story hour, Mac stood out like the proverbial bull in a china shop, not because he was breaking things, but because he was so, yes, that's right—male.

For this reason alone he didn't exactly blend into the scenery the way the rest of us did in our sweats and jeans and tired-looking faces. To make matters worse, Mac was immaculate, as was his son. Every week they would arrive on time, listen attentively, never make a mess; they put us to shame.

Though I wouldn't say we hated Mac, we didn't know what to do with him either. The fact that his wife—who works in publishing—is a hoot and-a-half to hang out with only made matters worse. It made even us feminist moms wish for a traditional division of labor. Why couldn't Mac go to work and Lucy stay home?

But that's not the way Mac and Lucy wanted it, so we just had to adjust, since frankly it was none of our business anyway. To his everlasting credit, Mac never seemed to care about fitting in. He was just trying to be a good dad, first to his son and then to his daughter when she showed up a few years later. He wasn't looking to make new friends, swap recipes, be a faux mom. He was never unfriendly, just sort of aloof.

Mac and I exchanged polite hellos for many years, on playgrounds, in parking lots, at birthday parties. We weren't quite friends, but we certainly weren't enemies, either. We were hospitable acquaintances. It was sometimes awkward, but mostly all right.

Things got easier as our kids got older; time has a way of doing that. Mac took up part-time coaching weekend soccer and after-school baseball. Not surprisingly, this more-traditional male role put us moms at ease. We knew how to relate to a man with a baseball in his hand better than we knew what to say to a guy pushing a stroller. (Shame on us for that.)

And yet, the best of Mac did not emerge until last spring at the final dance class our children attended together, along with 40 or so other third-graders.

Since it was the last event of the season, parents were invited to attend, and to dance with their children.

Mercilessly, the dance was scheduled for 4:30 in the afternoon, which made attending impossible for my husband, since his work day is rarely over before 7 p.m. Several dads did show up, much to my surprise, but I suspect a lot of them had to return to their offices afterward.

I didn't think it would matter much to any of the kids, whether or not their families showed up. Third-graders can be kind of oblivious. My mom, who came along to watch her grandchildren fox trot and cha-cha, ended up dancing with my daughter. They made a lovely couple.

I danced with my son; we won the mambo competition. I'm showing off by mentioning this fact, but you must understand this accomplishment means more to me than anything else I've ever done. I realize this makes me a very shallow person indeed, and I can live with that. After all, I know how to mambo well enough to win a prize. This sort of talent does not require depth.

I saw Mac out of the corner of my eye while I was dancing with my son. At first I assumed Lucy must be there, too, but a quick look around the room told me she was not. Neither were a lot of the other working moms who live in my town. Some older brothers were dancing with their sisters, some older sisters were dancing with their brothers. One or two mothers were dancing with their daughters, and as I said before, my daughter was dancing with my mother.

I have to admit that the children who had family members there were very pleased indeed, and the ones who didn't seemed a little droopy. The music was playing, the partners were swaying, and that's when I saw Mac. He was out on the dance floor, well-dressed as always, serious and sober, waltzing with his son. They were doing quite well.

They were both entirely masculine, completely unembarrassed, sort of in a world of their own. It's hard to imagine a more moving sight than this twosome: Winsome and Handsome showing off their steps to each other, and, if anyone cared to notice, to the town. I can't think of anyone else who could have pulled it off as unaffectedly as Mac did. He was so comfortable in his own skin, so fine with what he was doing that no one else seemed to notice. It was just as normal as me dancing with my son.

It reminded me that the best and most important part of being a parent is sometimes simply being there. Mac was being there for his son, just as he'd been there at library story hour. Only this time there was music, and it filled the room like lilacs in bloom. Or maybe it was just the aroma of love. And the best part of all was that Mac let his son lead.

Don't get me wrong. I still don't quite know what to do with Mac. He'll never be my girlfriend. But I'm sure glad he lives in my town.

Coaching softball

If someone had to describe me using only one word, that word would probably not be "athletic." Nor would it be "lithe," though possibly "limber." I have also, as yet, not been called a sports enthusiast. (Jocular, yes; a jock, no.) You get my drift. Verbal over manual dexterity, any day.

Don't remember playing softball when I was a girl. Kickball, dodge ball, basketball, yes. But all of those balls were hard. I should know: I was hit by them all. On a regular basis. There was also something called "underhanded baseball," I think, that we played, but that always sounded slightly nefarious to me. (I believe the name had to do with how the ball was pitched, literally, not metaphorically.)

But, you see, I have this daughter, and she's many of the things I never was but still aspire to be. The phrase "natural athlete" is the one that always comes to thought, followed by "graceful," "winsome," and "tough little monkey." She hits, she throws, she gets it. And, most amazing of all, she wanted me—the far-reaching but not-very-far-throwing writer in the family—to help coach her softball team this year. How could I say no? Are you joking? This is better than a PEN award.

I live in a town that is pretty much run by women—just ask any man on his way to the train station and he'll tell you the same. Our mayor's a woman, several of our village trustees are women, and quite a few board of education members are women, too. The men get a seat or two here and there, but if a woman walks in, he has to get up and give it over. That's just the way it is in this town, except in one regard—after-school sports. After-school sports have always been a dad's domain, and you could say we women are greedy not to leave things as they are. So I'll say it; we're greedy.

Last year, a mom friend of mine was the assistant coach of her son's baseball team. She caught a lot of grief, but she didn't mind. Before she was a mom, she was a cop in the Bronx. She can take care of herself.

This year, another mom friend of mine decided she wanted to be head coach of her daughter's softball team. I said I'd be her assistant coach, if she promised not to laugh at me too much. The girls on our team are your typical third-and fourth-graders—all gangly and giggles. A few good players, but even those were unreliable because they'd had no experience.

We call our team The Butterflies, not exactly a name to strike terror in the hearts of opposing teams. We have two other assistant coaches: a woman who has three sons and teaches yoga (she gets the girls to breathe deeply before each game and practice), and a mom who has a daughter who runs like a gazelle…on roller skates.

There's also one very nice but discombobulated-looking dad coach, who occasionally shows up when his work permits. He mainly stands on the third-base line, shaking his head in disbelief.

Moms definitely do not coach the way dads do. Dads are distinct. Moms are blurry. And we aren't trying to act like men, either. We call the girls "honey" and "sweetie," and we tell them not to worry, they'll get a hit next time. We hug and kiss a lot. We are soft. But then this is a girl's world. This is softball. We figure we're supposed to be soft.

Our first game we lost, badly: 27 to 13, more or less. But we practiced, we ran around the bases till our sides hurt, and we hit and threw and ran some more.

The next game we also lost, but not by much. A few runs, maybe three. Another practice, fewer water breaks, more focus.

Then came game No. 3. A tie. It would have gone on indefinitely, but another game was scheduled, so we had to yield the field. And then the breakthrough came. We won—by one run. Then we won again. And again.

It was amazing. I say "we" because the coaches feel so connected to the team—and because the head coach pitches every game. That's the way it is in elementary-school softball. The other coaches run, hit, and field with the team, too—during practice.

Our last game was rained out. Who knows how the season will end? But I know it doesn't matter, because our little caterpillars have emerged as butterflies.

And so, I suspect, have their mothers.

The logic in a stay-at-home mom's head of steam

I'd been working on this theory, building up a head of steam like some old freight train. I was just about ready to start whining on paper about how working moms take advantage of the moms like me who choose to stay at home. How we, the stay-at-home—or leisure—moms, are in fact the village it takes to raise a child, especially the child of the working mom. We fill in for the field trips, we do the carpooling and last-minute pickups when someone gets stuck at the office. We are the glue that holds it all together.

I had all sorts of jokes to make, at the working mom's expense. I figured, hey, she has a job, she can afford a little ribbing. My stay-at-home-mom friends agreed with me, too. Clearly we two groups of women get along about as well as the Jets and the Sharks in "West Side Story."

Then Susan had to go and mess everything up.

Let me tell you a few things about my good friend Susan. To begin with, she's smart, also funny, and she and her husband are doing a first-rate job of raising a great kid.

Susan offered to take my kids to the mall with her daughter and buy them all dinner at the food court. She was going to the mall to buy a going-away present for a summer intern at her office. Yep, that's right, Susan is a working mom with a very big job at a very big company. So Susan was doing what most stay-home mothers do for each other—helping out another mom, unasked, without expectation of reciprocation.

She wasn't making a grand gesture, just a kind one that enabled me to sneak a little more writing time in my very nice but overcrowded day. Suddenly my high horse seemed like a pretty low pony.

There's a schism between moms who work and moms who don't. (Yeah, I know, we're all working mothers, but you know what I mean—the ones with paychecks versus the ones without.) And we've got to bridge that schism.

This sea change in me got me thinking about all the times some mothers who stay home still find the opportunity to impose on other stay-at-home moms like me, without giving it a thought.

Then I thought about all the juggler moms I know who somehow manage to get to their afternoon work meeting and still be on the bus for the morning field trip to the ballet—working moms who lie about where they are, risk their jobs, to be with their kids.

I've long been aware that the way the world works, women are made to feel they've made the wrong choice no matter what they do, or don't do. If you stay home, you're not fulfilling your potential (as if potential can only be filled in an office situation). If you work, you're missing out on raising your child. Well, some women have to work, and that's all there is to it.

I have very strong opinions about women staying home to be with their kids until they go to college. I see this as, if not my job, my commitment. But Susan made me realize I'd forgotten something very important, even essential—that before we were moms, we were sisters; that women are supposed to support each other. That's what feminism is all about, supporting each others' choices even if we don't agree with them—and especially if we don't agree with them.

Obviously, I feel the best choice a woman can make is to stay home with her children. But that doesn't give me the right to be self-righteous. We often have to make choices of necessity—usually economic.

Many women would love to stay home with their kids, but can't because either they're single parents or they need two paychecks to make ends meet.

Many women don't want to stay home with their kids, and to be honest, those are the women I have a problem with. No one put a gun to their heads and said "Procreate!" Somehow, someway, someday soon, we've got to learn to talk about the money. It divides the women who can afford to stay home with their children, and those who simply can't.

But there's another, more insidious, side to this cash-flow problem we're all in the throes of. There's a money obsession gripping this country like an ill-fitting shoe (see "Survivor" or "Big Brother," or better yet, don't), that makes people think they need these overburdened, fast-track lives that often leave their children in the dust. It's too easy to shrug it off by saying, it's the culture, as if one were referring to something that lurks over there somewhere.

People, I have seen The Culture, and it is us.

But maybe just the fact that Susan and I are such good friends, even though we're in different camps, as it were, is proof that things are not so grim.

If the Jets and the Sharks could learn to get along—and after all the dancing and rumbling, they did leave the abandoned playground as friends, remember?—then maybe all of us moms can play nice too.

Around and around the mommy track

The public school in our town has a quarter-mile athletic track used by all the students from kindergarten through 12th grade. But everybody knows that the track's not really for the kids. Oh no. The track belongs to the moms like me who stay home with the kids.

Every morning we deliver our children to their classrooms and then we go around and around and around in circles, savoring every step. It's a perfect metaphor for our collective lives. To an outsider we don't appear to be getting anywhere. But we are; we're just taking a circuitous route. At the very least, we're going nowhere together. Walking shoes, white socks, black leggings, sweatshirt (in the winter), or baggy T-shirt (in the summer) is the outfit de rigueur. Dark glasses are recommended, but not required. Caps are good, too, especially the nondescript baseball variety. But only if you have straight hair. A baseball cap on me looks like haberdashery on a caribou. You can't really tell who's making fun of whom, but there sure is a lot of pointing and laughing going on between my hair and my hat.

Some of us listen to music on headphones. Some of us engage in light conversation, our version of commuter gab. The rest of us would rather walk alone, reclaiming the lost art of thinking. You know, that thing we used to do with our thoughts, before we had children.

Occasionally a brave-hearted man shows up, but we don't let him stand in our way. We just keep right on talking and walking and rocking, like we're the real planets and he's just some meteor passing through. The Mr. Mommy track this isn't. Eventually the guys give up and go to work.

I know someone who during the worst winter months goes around the track in a mink coat. It's not exactly politically correct, and it certainly isn't what you'd call a sports look, but I'm sure it's very toasty. The track is, after all, located several inches (on the Rand McNally map) above the Mason-Dixon Line. She probably doesn't mind if we find her peculiar, so long as we don't hurl turnips at her head. (Come to think of it, hurling turnips would make us peculiar, wouldn't it?)

The mink with the running shoes gives a whole new meaning to the phrase "warm-up suit." I imagine the weight of the coat does burn off a few more calories than a mere parka or windbreaker.

One very chilly early spring morning, I saw the mink mom walking around the track, followed by another woman who was wearing low black-leather heels, a shoulder bag, and a black wool coat over a business suit. The two of them looked as though they were vying for a grant from the Ministry of Silly Walks. After two laps, one of them hobbled off toward the train station and the other headed home.

Fortunately, it will be summer soon. Uniformity of dress will return, the one infraction being black shorts. (The preferred color is white.) Then the only thing I'll have to worry about is the humidity making my hair so big that the cap on my head explodes.

A reluctant would-be general in my school's army of moms

I love having a reason for hanging out at school. I enjoy watching the kids in the hall, mine and everyone else's. And I love having an official purpose, so that no one can stare at me wondering what's she doing here? Well, yeah, they can do that, but they can't kick me out, at least not on Mondays. Monday is my day at the school's Publishing Center.

The Publishing Center is where you can quietly word-process short stories written by schoolchildren aged 5 through 11, and make covers for the books these stories will comprise. It's not very challenging, and I mean that in a good way. It's just a little way of helping out.

I'm one of the head honchos or, rather, "honchettes." I even have the key. I get to lock up. I'm very good at locking up. I haven't forgotten to once all year. My book covers leave a lot to be desired (covers require patience and a willingness to iron), my laminating skills are mediocre, and I'm a bit askew on the hole-punching machine. My main selling point is that I always show up.

But now, through some suburban version of the Peter Principle, I've been asked to run the Publishing Center next year. I should be flattered, except that I suspect the Elementary School Council's search for the perfect leader is alphabetical, and the mothers whose last names both begin with "B" have already turned down the assignment. That leaves me and the mom whose last name starts with "S."

I think the "S" mom is the far better candidate. She's the one who noticed someone had walked off with the scissors. She's the one who got not one but two replacement pairs from the school store, and got a receipt so she could be readily reimbursed. She's also the one who attached undetachable labels to the scissors that say "Publishing Center." She has an eye for details. She pays attention, and she enjoys talking on the phone. That's a real plus for the job, since whoever runs the Publishing Center has to—you know—talk to people. About ordering supplies, about getting more moms to volunteer, about scheduling and rescheduling. The "S" mom even called to let me know the scissors were missing and maybe I should bring in my own pair from home. (Of course I couldn't. Someone's walked off with our pair, too.)

Had it been left to me, the Publishing Center would still be scissorless and work would be piling up and I'd be—oh, I don't know—typing up stories, I guess, and avoiding the book-binding part. Or else I'd be thinking of alternative ways to cut paper and fabric. Burning long holes in them with the iron. Biting them apart with my teeth. Leaving it for the Tuesday mom to figure out. This is not the m.o. of someone who can run something, except maybe into the ground.

I'm hoping the Elementary Council members will see the error of their ways and pass me over for promotion. Because if they don't, I may actually end up running the Publishing Center next year, simply because I forgot to get back to them to say no I can't/won't do it. And that would be sad for everyone, especially for me, since it would mean I got the job by default, and it's my own d*** fault.

The mother lode of moms

One good thing about being a mother is that you get to have children, even if they're not always your own. Other than that, it may not be so great a career choice: long hours, lousy pay, no privacy, not much respect. A friend of mine says motherhood often feels like being wallpaper. I know what she means, having felt that way myself a little more than often. (Does anyone listen to wallpaper? I don't think so.)

But there's a lot to be said for wallpaper. Furniture may move, people may change, but wallpaper remains. You can count on it. It's a constant in a world of flux. That's what mothers are, or should be. The wallpaper we count on, the background of our lives.

I used to be in the forefront, the star of my own life. Now I'm a background, too. It's cool. The labor-intensive part of being wallpaper—I mean, a mother—doesn't last long. Stage 1 is pre-preschool: diapers, feedings, diapers, getting up in the middle of the night, diapers, strollers. Did I mention diapers?

Stage 2 is preschool. Still diapers, sometimes, but sipper cups replace bottles, and play dates begin (kids these days need a Filofax more than their moms do). Then there's library story hour, naps (maybe), still not much sleep; for you, that is.

Finally, Stage 3: school! More time for you…to volunteer for the PTA, to become chauffeur-mom (cap not required), to help with homework, and, yes, get a little more sleep, at last. But if you have more children, it's déjà vu all over again. And again.

I love the phrase "full-time mother." Like there's such a thing as a part-time mom? Folks, this ain't no hobby, and it's not getting any easier. You make it up as you go along, trying to keep your cool, your perspective, your car keys, and your sense of humor.

I've known some great moms. You could say I'm a mom collector. They've all been role models for me. From their examples I've cobbled together my best impression of what a mom should be. Most of the time I don't feel that I fill the bill. Fortunately, my kids haven't caught on yet.

Some of the best moms I've known didn't have kids of their own. It was simply their nature to nurture. I call them über-moms. Marque was one. She was a Sunday school teacher and a friend to anyone in need of mothering. She raised a lot of kids with her love. Some of them, like me, even had more-than-adequate moms to begin with. But I've always believed you can never have too many mothers.

Cami's an absentee mom. Absent from me that is, since she and her family moved to Winnetka. Before her husband got transferred she and I spent a lot of time together. Now that she lives several states away, she still provides me with a sounding board and a lot of solace. She also laughs at my jokes. She's raised two great boys. She likes other kids, too, but she always makes me feel like mine are a cut above. Clever woman. She is patient and undemanding. She's a constant source of common sense and good advice.

Then there my in town pals: Jan, Denise, Ellen, Deb, Kerry, to name but a few. We spend a lot of time together, occasionally having lunch, mostly watching our kids after school at the playground. Fortunately for all of us, our kids like each other. Because this is a very small town with an even smaller playground. Getting along is imperative.

My in town pals will gainsay me on this, but they are all very good at what they do, even though we've dubbed ourselves The Bad Mothers Club. (It's a joke, officer, really.) They provide me with the daily sanity check we front-line moms need to give each other. Such as, I'm not the only person on the planet (besides my husband) who thinks a seven-year-old should not see the movie "Titanic" or stay up until 10 on a school night. Or own his or her own Nintendo. Or a cell phone. We're talking seven now, not seventeen.

Ok, ok, I admit I lose points on the issue of Beanie Baby excess, but those things are cute and cuddly. And at $4.99 a beanie, kind of hard to resist. Besides, if my kids ever outgrow them I can sew them all together and make a large bean-bag couch. Ouch. Once I learn how to sew, that is.

Last but not least, there's my mom. You don't think I could leave her out, now, do you? Do you think I want to give up free baby-sitting? Free dinners? Free advice? Are you nuts? Come to think of it, that's what makes her such an extraordinary person, and mom. She does all this giving with no strings attached. She says she likes to do it. She's always been like this (at least as long as I've known her), so I've given up trying to figure it out. I'm just grateful to be on the receiving end.

For me, the best thing about being a mom is the bird's-eye view I get of what being a dad is all about. But that's another story.

Mom explains the muzzle-nuzzle rule

The other day it rained, and I was very, very crabby. It didn't help that the entire afternoon had been carefully crafted around my son's piano lesson, and that I had scolded him—gently, but firmly—about our being four minutes late to music school. For some, as in my son, dawdling is an art form. I extolled the virtues of punctuality as we first hurried to his class room, then waiting patiently for his teacher to arrive, only to find that his teacher had completely forgotten about his lesson—and all her other students, for that matter. In fact she had left town for the week. This I learned after listening to my son play "Chopsticks" for half an hour, and my daughter who'd come along for the ride, play something I'll call "Adagio for Elbows." I had planned to do errands while my son had his lesson. No lesson, no errands. Hurling two six-year-olds in and out of stores in the rain is more than I can muster. One six-year-old, yes. Two, out of the question. Errands can wait; six-year-olds won't, not when they travel in groups.

So though nothing had really gone wrong, nothing had really gone right, either, and I kind of sort of lost my perspective. No self-respecting journalist would have covered this story. I can just see the headline: "Teacher's Unmentioned Vacation Has Tragic Consequences—An Afternoon in Shambles!" And, sad to say, by the end of the day I was not voted Ms. Congeniality. Not by a long shot. I'm amazed my family didn't put me out with the cat, the only possible explanation being that we don't have a cat. Crabbiness is a little like crabgrass—same root. Same route, too. Crabbiness tends to take over the landscape of the mind, coloring everything dull and dismal. It's a weed, so by nature it's a spoilsport. I should know, I've worked this garden before.

But the next day, it was sunny and spring-like and it seemed as if all the trees had sneaked into their fine greenery overnight. The kids got up without protest, and we made it to school better than on time, five minutes early. And then I got to do those unattended to errands, nothing important, just the small stuff that needs to get done or our lives fall apart. Grocery store, post office, other necessary incidentals. And as the day went on, I realized I had been the recipient of several small but significant kindnesses.

For starters, the book my husband and I have been waiting and waiting and waiting for finally came into the bookstore a day earlier than its so-called publication date, and the booksellers let me have it anyway. They did make me promise not to tell anyone, but they didn't specifically rule out writing about it, so I think I'm in the clear.

Then the young man at the bagel store gave me four raspberry jam-filled croissants for free because he knows I love chocolate croissants and he feels bad about not carrying them any more. And I've never even complained about it. No, really I haven't. Occasionally I even buy bagels at the bagel store. Finally, the teenager at the beverage mart loaded all seven cases of seltzer into my car without my even asking him to. (Why seven cases? We like to buy in bulk. We really like seltzer.)

And I knew the piano teacher would eventually return, all apologetic and repentant, and in the meantime there's always practicing at home. It's not like our son is booked on a concert tour. He only knows three songs. But I was struck, figuratively of course, by the rampant niceness that met me at every turn. It may have had something to do with better weather and spring in the air, but I suspect it also had more to do with clearing out the crabbiness. All that merciful kindness was probably there the day before. Goodness always is, rain or shine. Sometimes I growl too loudly to notice. That's usually when my kids are smart enough to give me an unexpected hug and a kiss.

Some days, moms just need to be muzzled. And some days we need to be nuzzled. But kids, if your mom is in a really crabby mood, first muzzle, then nuzzle.

To speak of mothers

To speak of breakfast is to speak of mothers. Breakfast is that meal which separates the sensible from the slightly possessed, the on-the-mark mothers, from those who function above and beyond the call of duty.

I have always felt my mother fell into the second category for two reasons. First of all she always made my breakfast every morning. Secondly, she still is, by her own admission, mind you, "not very good in the morning." She bumps into furniture, forgets where she puts things, like the English muffins ("They're in the toaster? How'd they get in there?") This has nothing at all to do with advancing age. By 9 a.m. she's as sharp as a tack and ready to rock'n'roll. Always has been, always will be. But before that first cup of tea or coffee, well, don't get me started 'cause you won't get her started either.

But this lack of early luster in no way incapacitates her culinary skills. A brilliant conversationalist at 7 a.m. she is not. Julia Child she is.

At first I thought, like all self-centered children, nothing of this at all. I assumed that breakfast came with the warranty, along with a bed and new toys. However as soon as I was old enough to hold a decent conversation with my schoolmates—about age five—I discovered that not everybody's mother got up and made breakfast like mine did. Certainly not every day and rarely with such imaginative offerings fit for the morning menu at The Plaza Hotel. French toast, hot cereal, eggs and bacon, waffles, pancakes. Not all at the same time, of course, but that was the epicurean cycle of my mornings. No wonder I went to school happy! For roughly 90 seconds I felt like a social outcast, ashamed of my well fed status. This guilt pang lasted about as long as my hunger pangs usually did at the breakfast table.

Craftily I began to ask my mother unassuming questions like, "Did your mother make you breakfast every morning?" Sleuthing my way to the bottom of this delicious conundrum. And as it turned out, her mother made her and her sisters breakfast with equal aplomb and regularity, and I might also add, with equal lack of additional alertness. A pattern was emerging. Perhaps there was a genetic inclination in all McKenzie women to go that extra mile, meal wise. But to believe that biology is destiny is one instance is to tacitly endorse far less palatable issues, hinged on the same premise.

So maybe she was one of those happy homemakers whose only fulfillment was lodged somewhere between the oven and the refrigerator. But this postulation crumbled when I recalled that the easiest way to put a smile on my mother's face is to say those three little words—"Let's eat out."

Finally I doffed my deerstalker hat. Who ever heard of a nine year old girl named Sherlock anyway? I seized upon the obvious and just asked her, "Why do you make my breakfast for me every morning?"

The answer was so simple it went right over my head. "Because," she said, "I like to."

Then one morning several years later it all became clear to me. I was living at home again, no longer off to school, but to a job that required my showing up at work at the altogether ridiculous hour of 6:15 a.m. It was midwinter and I was old enough to have voted in two presidential elections and tall enough to reach the kitchen cabinets without having to stand on tiptoe. Certainly capable of fending for myself. That morning, which seemed more like the middle of the night, I stumbled downstairs to greet the day with a snarl, only to find my mother, equally uneffusive, sitting at the breakfast table with two places set. There were promising aromas wafting in the air. Could it be? Yes, food! In another three hours she would stage a repeat performance with my father, though for the second show she usually only joined in on the orange juice. Which explains how she's kept her girlish figure, if you get my drift.

As we sat there, two women, bonded by so much more than meals, it occurred to me that someday I would want to be on the other side of this scene. I would want to be the one who made the breakfast for my probably none-too-glorious morning glory. It's not that I subscribe to the determining power of heredity, but there are such things as trends.

And now that I am a mother whose breakfast skills are at best fair to middling, I keep hoping for the day one of my children asks me with suspicions brimming in their eyes, why in the name of reason I get up every morning to make or at least assemble their breakfast. Because the answer is on the tip of my tongue. As my mother said to me, and hers to her, because I like to.

The best mothers seem to know instinctively how to nurture their children. My mother's really no better than the rest, I guess. She's just a lot more literal.

A dance to the music of life

It was my turn to be hostess/mom at the Barclay classes. The Barclay classes took over for Miss Covington's, as the time-honored teach-your-child-to-dance-and-some-manners while-we're-at-it tradition in my town. The hoi polloi in Beverly Hills where I grew up would have called it a cotillion, which it isn't. It has nothing to do with debutantes. It has every thing to do with manners and social graces. It is open to all children from third to sixth grade, though boys are especially welcome for reasons all too obvious. There may be equality in the 21st century, but most boys still prefer T-shirts and jeans to white shirts and slacks. Not to mention the jacket and the tie.

In other words, most boys still have to be dragged there by their metaphorical ears, bribed or threatened or cajoled into attending. My son is no exception, though he's a very good dancer. My daughter says she doesn't want to go, but I know she's just pretending. Though she also prefers wearing T-shirts and jeans, her party clothes have a decided advantage over her brother's. Hers sparkle and twirl; his are just scratchy.

The classes meet twice a month from September until March. Mothers like me (if there is such a thing) can volunteer to host a class, which means sitting at a table with a list of children's names and checking them in as they arrive. Some of these children I've known since they were 3, so it's amusing to say, "And your name is…?" to kids I used to strap into car seats. They play along, though, saying their names clearly enough to hear, but not loud enough to shout. That's part of the purpose of the class: eye contact, speaking distinctly, smiling. It used to be called acting human, now it's more like humane.

Then the moms (there are two for each class) shake hands hello with the children, and shake hands goodbye at the end. The class is only an hour long. The third-graders meet from 4 until 5, the fourth-graders from 4:15 to 5:15, the fifth-graders from 5:30 to 6:30, and (gasp!) the sixth-graders have a veritable soiree from 6:45 to 7:45. Quelle surprise!

My kids are third-graders, they dance at 4. They tell me it's torture, and they make monster faces at me, but I don't care, and neither do the other mothers. For us, it's the high point of the month. We love everything the Barclay classes represent: not only the learning to dance to live music (a drummer and a piano player), the faltering steps of a cha-cha or box step, but the gentle chiseling away of playground rowdiness and the occasional emergence of something from a bygone era—manners.

During the hour, the children forget themselves, or rather become themselves, sweet and silly and, well, polite. It's enough to make you cry. I often do, and not because my kids are wooly mammoths in their spare time. It's just that this arcane custom seems to bring out the best in them.

I'm not sure why the girls wear white gloves. I only know I like it. Even the mothers have to scrounge up a pair when they serve as hostesses, though mine were given away to a girl who came without hers and was considering painting her hands white in hopes of blending in. Not that it would have been necessary. The people who run the classes are disciplined, but good and kind, not despotic tyrants. After all, you can't teach good manners if you don't have them yourself.

Once a girl came in a lovely dress, but without her party shoes. The girl had come with a friend, who unfortunately is a boy. I say "unfortunately" because he couldn't lend her a pair of shoes. But his mom assured the girl that she looked marvelous with her blue sneakers peering out from under her taffeta skirt. "Just hold your head up high and smile," the mother told her. I held my breath as I watched her walk in, wondering if she'd be turned away at the door. She was not. That wouldn't have been good manners either; that would have been snobbery. There is a decided difference between the two.

Allison is a mother I've known for a very long time, since her son was 2 and before her daughter, Grace, was born. Grace is in kindergarten now. If you were casting a movie called "The Adorable Tomboy," Grace would get the lead. She wears pigtails and overalls. She has the face of an angel and the upper cut of a prize fighter. She doesn't start fights, but she's been known to finish them.

The day I was hostess, Grace was there with her mom. They were watching Grace's brother Luke dance with a girl who was slightly taller than he. Luke was doing quite well, so well that it inspired Allison and Grace to dance by themselves in the hall. While the third-graders cha cha cha'd to "Strangers in the Night," Grace and her mom took turns twirling each other, just out of view, so Luke never knew and was therefore not embarrassed.

But I saw them dancing, mother and daughter. It only lasted a moment or two. But it was lovely. It was lyrical too. That's the effect that the Barclay classes have. They make the mundane magical.

We could have danced all night

It was two weeks before my eighth-grade graduation. My dad, a screenwriter, was working on a movie in Ireland. It was becoming clear to all of us—my mother, my father, and I—that he wouldn't be home in time to see me graduate, home being southern California. Naturally, I was disappointed, but I understood that it wasn't his choice; it was his job.

The hard part for both of us was the fact that he'd miss the father-daughter dance, the highlight of the graduation-night party. Dad said he'd make it up to me somehow, and I should go and have a good time. Dance with my friends. Reluctantly, I agreed. This wasn't my first dance solo, you see. At my second-grade ballet recital I'd been forced to do a pas de deux à une, if you will, when my partner was sidelined by a tummy ache. He was fine the next day. I was embarrassed for a week. There's a home movie of it somewhere, me leaping boldly if not gracefully into the arms of the invisible man. Very post-modern. Very weird. I wasn't about to do that again. I'd just sit out the father-daughter part.

Graduation day came, and I got my hair done in that goofy way teenage girls did then, and sometimes do today. Bangs down to my eyeballs. Hair long and blow-dried bone straight. And lacquered. A garland of silk daisies circled my head. I wore a white dress not nearly short enough to suit my tastes, but as short as the principal would allow. With sheer white nylons and white patent-leather shoes, I looked like a love child student nurse.

One-hundred and twenty of us crowded into bleachers on the school's front lawn that afternoon. There was talk of carrying the torch, going out into the world, making a difference. (But we were only going half a mile away to the high school.)

Graduation was followed by a dinner for the graduates and their families. After dinner, the dance began: two hours of rock 'n' roll. The last blast before the next leap. My mom left after dinner, as did all the parents, except chaperones. She said she'd pick me up at 9:30 and we'd go out for ice cream. She winked and said, "Have fun!" And I did. We were all bright, shiny, happy kids, relieved to find we still had some childhood left after all. We danced hard and happy. Something was ending, and something was about to begin. Nothing to do but hold on and enjoy the ride.

At 9:15, the DJ announced that the fathers had arrived and it was time for them to find their daughters on the dance floor. Time's up, I thought, and started to leave, feeling like Cinderella would have felt if she'd left the ball before dancing with the prince.

Then, looking up, I saw him standing there. Not my father—my godfather. He was grinning, and he was making his way toward me. Dad had called him and asked him to fill in, which he was only too happy to do. He was my dad's best friend after all, and his wife, Marge, was my mom's best friend. She and my mom stood on the sidelines watching with matching smiles. I raced toward him. He hugged me and said, "Shall we dance?" And then it hit me. There was one little problem. My godfather wasn't some nice old klutz. He was Gower Champion.

Maybe you've heard of him? The dancer? The choreographer, the director of Broadway shows? The guy who had so many Tony awards on his desk they looked like coasters?

True, he was a father, but here, surrounded by stodgy bankers and doctors in business suits, he looked like a date. He was wearing white pants and a blue cashmere sweater, loafers with no socks. And I was about to dance with him. I felt faint.

Sure, I could do the steps I saw on "Soul Train" and "American Band Stand." But this was serious. The father-daughter dance was all foxtrots and waltzes. Dad and I could have stumbled through it, laughing as we took turns stepping on each other's toes. But dancing? With Gower Champion? I was going to make a complete fool of myself.

But then he circled my back with his arm and, placing my clammy right hand in his (which was warm and rock steady), he said, "Just relax, and follow me."

The music started. Fred Astaire singing "The Way You Look Tonight." We glided, we twirled, we moved like twin swans. Gower was a good enough dancer for both of us. All I had to do was keep breathing. Somehow I managed.

I leaned my head against him. He whispered, "You're doing fine." By the end of the song I was soaring. It was better than being Ginger Rogers. Better than dancing with Fred. It was dancing with Gower. It was pure and simple. And yet it was a new step, a dance into adolescence.

Then the music changed to rock 'n' roll. This was a recent addition to the tradition, basically to embarrass the dads. The rest of them stumbled and sweated to The Rolling Stones' "Satisfaction" while the daughters laughed and blushed at their fathers' foolishness.

Not me. I was dancing with Gower. He could out-dance most of the boys in my class. He was in a class all his own. No, they didn't form a circle around us and watch us groove (this wasn't the movies; it just felt like it was). But I did feel more than a few furtive glances shot our way as we shimmied and shook. My, oh my!

Mom, Marge, Gower, and I all went out for ice cream after the dance ended. Marge gave me a garnet necklace—I still have it. And from then on, I always felt I was partly Marge and Gower's daughter, too.

Finally, we said good night. Marge and Gower walked arm in arm to their car, and Mom and I got into ours. He turned one last time as he drove away, to smile and wave and hug me with his eyes. My heart danced as he did.

A hometown hero from Hollywood

I love the town I live in. For one thing, it's a village, only one square mile big. It's full of flowering trees and gardens. It has a library and a Haagen-Dazs. Plus, if you live here long enough it's like that TV series "Cheers"—everybody knows your name. And if not your name, at least your face. People smile and say hello.

If you're a mom like me, you can see the same people (and by "people," I mean moms) three or four times a day: at school, the supermarket, the video store, the bank. After the third run-in, you're allowed to act as if you don't see one another. But if I had to come up with the single reason why I love this place above all other places, the answer would be: Gwen Verdon.

You wouldn't think that living in the same town as Gwen Verdon, who was a really big star in the 1950s and '60s, would be such a big deal to me, since I grew up in southern California. I saw as many actors, dancers, and movie stars as most people see policemen, teachers, or—I don't know—waiters. Actually, most of the waiters I saw growing up were actors. At least that's what they told me.

So seeing celebrities shouldn't be such a big deal. But what can I say? Gwen Verdon is different. She is a goddess walking the earth. Maybe she has this effect on me because I first saw her dance when I was a child no older than my own daughter is now. It was a movie version of the hit Broadway show "Damn Yankees."

Miss Verdon was a whole lot of wow: sultry, snazzy, funny, but also vulnerable, tender, and boy oh boy could she dance. I wished with all my heart that I could look, act, and dance the way she did when I grew up. I didn't get my wish, but I got a close second: I get to see her when I'm doing my errands.

Now, I'm not implying that Miss Verdon is jeté-ing down the main road in my town, picking up her dry cleaning wearing fishnet tights and a leotard. Miss Verdon dresses like the rest of us, in sweaters and trousers—and occasionally, in colder months, a cape. She looks regal, but not off-putting. Now that I'm older and so is she, I want even more to be like her—classy and sassy, cool (as in hip, not as in cold) and still working, but also doing my own shopping like it's no big deal. That's the way she danced—like scorching the earth with her feet was no big deal. For me, she epitomizes the fact that, famous or not, life goes on and stuff needs to get done. She gives that fact more than pizzazz, she gives it hope.

I've learned to cultivate a sly acknowledging grin whenever I see her and our eyes happen to meet. I don't want to invade her privacy, or appear to be a stalker. But I also want to make sure that she knows that I know who she is. More than that: I want her to know that seeing her has made my day. Why, you ask?

Because of all the places she could live—Malibu, Monterey, San Francisco, Santa Fe—she chose here. As I did. It makes my choice seem less random, more special. My husband and I chose this town because it has a great school for our kids and it's an easy commute into work for him.

But what do I get out of the deal? I, who could live anywhere so long as there's a typewriter/word processor/piece of paper and pen. What do I get? I get Gwen. I get my own private joke that I share with myself. Or to quote a song from that long-ago musical, I get proof that all you really need in life is "a little brains, a little talent, with an emphasis on the latter."

If you're scratching your head and thinking, "Who's Gwen Verdon?" Well, all I can say is shame on you. It's a darn good thing you don't live in my town. You'd miss all the best sights.

The Beatles, as they were meant to be

Recently, my husband and I have been receiving a lot of "The Beatles Anthology" CDs, usually from friends much older or much younger than we are. These friends assume we pine for the music of our early youth, much the way tourists assume Hawaiians pine for ukuleles and palm trees.

These CDs have been remastered, digitally tweaked, and in all manner of ways improved so that listening to the Fab Four now has an aura of aural pomposity, entirely out of sync with the songs I used to lip-sync to. It's a little depressing. The tunes I found so riveting that I couldn't turn off the radio while one was playing now waft from our state-of-the-art sound system as so much amplified wifwaf.

We scratch our heads and wonder what the fuss was all about. Then we switch to another CD, usually Coltrane, Brahms, or Dylan. These three stand the test of time because one was a jazz giant, one was a classical genius, and the last guy was, and is, and ever will be a poet of the soul. Forget the voice (if you must); read the lyrics. And we sigh because we used to think of John, Paul, George, and Ringo in the same terms (well, John anyway).

But then the other morning I heard the faint sounds of "Twist and Shout" coming from another part of the house. It gave me goose bumps, the way it did the first time I heard John Lennon croak out that song. And much to my surprise, I sang along, remembering every word, every note, every inflection. The song grew louder. I turned and found our six-year-old daughter grinning, holding her multi-colored, child-sized cassette player, the one with the sing-along microphone and carrying handle. From its red-plastic center emanated that glorious sound.

I could tell she liked the tape. It was one I had bought for her on a whim years before, when she was maybe one and I was very tired of Raffi. And it sounded so good because it sounded the way it had when it first came squishing out of an old transistor radio or a Neanderthal monaural hi-fi. I know I'm sounding dangerously like a geezer, or perhaps a geezette, but I really think I'm on to something here. The Beatle sound is supposed to be raw, compressed, kind of scratchy. Listened to under optimum conditions, with the precision of a microscope, it's heard for what it really is—only rock-and-roll. But when played on a cheap cassette player, it comes alive again. It's got soul.

The point here is that the guy was wrong who wrote, "The unexamined life is not worth living." Yes I know is was Socrates, but it's still Greek to me. Think of all the memoirs we'd have been spared if only he'd misplaced his pad and pencil. I mean, sure, if you're sitting around in a toga surrounded by a gaggle of adoring acolytes who hang on your every word, go ahead and examine your life till the cows come home. Examine the cows' lives while you're at it. But for the rest of us, the unexamined life is sometimes a lot easier to live than the examined one, especially if you have kids and car payments. The overly examined anything tends to take the fun out of life. And leaves you with, well, a lot of over-amplified wif-waf.

The music played on. My daughter and I did the Twist while we did the dishes. How could I dance with another when I saw her standing there?

Still counting on 'Sesame Street'

In the fall of 1969, something unusual was happening every afternoon in the Beverly Hills High School library. I know because I was there. The facility had just been hooked up to something called the Information Retrieval System, a sort of precursor to the electronic age that lay ahead. It allowed students to watch the local public television station from small cubicles, each of which contained a TV screen and a set of head phones.

A myriad of programming was available. Documentaries on everything from Alaskan wolves to Vietnam. Programs that taught languages—Spanish, Hebrew, Japanese. But only one show got any real viewing audience from the teenage habitués of the library, and these were mostly large athletic-looking seniors. They would sit in their individual carrels, happily oblivious to their surroundings, shouting out a song that went "1,2,3,4,5,6,7,8,9,10!" They were watching this new show called "Sesame Street."

Obviously the intended audience was children slightly younger, by oh, maybe 15 years. But right from the start, when "Sesame Street" debuted Nov. 10, 1969, everybody got with and loved the program. It melded and welded learning and having fun into one big, loud, cross-cultural mishmash. It showed America as a land of many colors—red, white, and brown.

In the fast approaching 40 years it's been on the air, we the viewing audience have watched the "Sesame Street" family grow and change as our own families have grown and changed. Right from the start, it had an urban appeal. It showed kids living and learning in a magical, mythical place filled with talking monsters like Grover, and Cookie, and eventually Elmo; plus my two personal favorites, the chronically cranky Oscar the Grouch and the sublimely angst-ridden Telly. "Sesame Street" is a place that looks more than a little like that magical, mythical place called New York City, where occasionally you might run into a cranky and angst-full character who's not made of brightly colored faux fur.

I won't tell you how old I was when I first started watching "Sesame Street" back in 1969. No, I wasn't a high-school senior, but I had known my ABCs and colors, and how to count from 1 to 10 for quite some time. However that didn't keep me or any of my friends from tuning in most afternoons to see what was happening on that now famous front stoop, or in Mr. Hooper's store, to see who was making a guest appearance that day.

Everyone—from the New York Mets to the cast of "Upstairs, Downstairs," to Isaac Stern to Robin Williams to, most recently, the rock band called The Goo Goo Dolls—eventually gets to "Sesame Street." Because, after all, celebrities have children, and what better way to impress your child than to do a time step or shuffle off to Buffalo with Snuffleupagus? And those who don't have children were once children (or act like badly behaved children, in the case of The Goo Goo Dolls). The point being somewhere deep down inside of us all there still lives a wide-eyed three-year-old.

My own kids are now too old to be part of the "Sesame Street" target audience, which I assume is between the ages of 2 and 5. They were "Sesame Street" maniacs in their pre-school days, but now they have a hard time admitting the guilty pleasure of hearing Bert and Ernie sing a duet. That's ok; they're still too young to understand that no one is ever too old for "Sesame Street." Giving up this show is about as likely as growing taller than Big Bird. Face it. It's not gonna happen.

First know thyself—then copy
Meg Ryan

There's nothing funny about getting a good haircut. I should know. I've laughed my way through some pretty bad ones.

So I was riveted by an item in The New York Times about a hair salon that, before giving a haircut, gives its clients a written quiz, an actual, five-page, written test, chock-full of multiple-choice questions about the kind of car you drive, the sort of vacation you like to take, what kind of restaurant you frequent—basically a lot of questions about money and how much of it you have.

What? Is this a haircut or a credit check? And does this mean that now, even a simple snip and curl requires studying and making the grade?

The more I thought about it, the more interested and the more alarmed I became. Interested, because I would go to practically any length to obtain a hairdo that doesn't make me look like Elvis on a windy day. Alarmed, because it seemed like once again, "My Generation" was going out of its way to complicate and obfuscate the simple. Why do I need to take a quiz? What if I get some of the answers wrong? Will I be given a derogatory bouffant?

But the lure of trivial introspection drew me on. The idea here is the better you know yourself, the better your haircut will be.

So I boarded the train early one morning, and headed for Manhattan. I got to the salon ahead of time and found, much to my amazement that the man who was going to cut my hair—Benoit—was ready and waiting for me. Wow. I'd forgotten that to people living in New York City, on time means being five minutes early.

Benoit looked at me, he looked at my hair. He nodded, he smiled. He asked a few questions that I didn't understand—partly because when I'm a little bit nervous, I don't listen very well, and partly because of his rather thick French accent. At first, I was afraid I was about to have my hair cut by Inspector Clouseau. But then I relaxed, there were no bandages on his fingers, he obviously knew what he was doing.

But he didn't seem the least bit interested in the quiz. I had already asked the receptionist for it—she had smiled, sort of (a New York City smile is sort of a quick, but pleasant smirk). The answers would let me know whether or not I was high, medium, or low maintenance. I already knew the answer: low, extremely low.

How often do I work out? (Do they mean how often do I think I work out? Or how often do I actually work out?) What magazine do I like best? (I had to write in The New Yorker, feeling I couldn't be defined by the given choices—Vogue, Glamour, Reader's Digest, National Geographic). How long do I expect my career to last? (Which career? Writer? Mother? Household purchasing agent? Filing clerk? Finder of all things lost or misplaced?) Exactly 50 minutes, one shampoo, and a haircut later, I didn't look so bad. The quiz confirmed what I already knew: I don't like to spend a lot of time on my hair, my role model is more Meg Ryan than Gwyneth Paltrow—definitely not Cher. But who said anything about wanting or needing a role model?

I asked the shop's proprietor, a highly coiffed woman named Kim, what exactly the point of the quiz is. Do we really want to keep identifying with movie stars? Quite the opposite, she explained. Define your lifestyle first, then as a sort of visual shorthand, you can pick the perfect media type. High Maintenance? (Soap opera diva Susan Lucci.) Low Maintenance? (Jada Pinkett Smith crew cut.) The point being, I guess, that first you have to know yourself before you can steal someone else's look.

So I guess I'm in favor of giving the quiz.

But I don't think it's the client who should take it. It's the stylists, and the first question should be: Do you know how to give a good hair cut? If they answer "Yes, I do," then you can ask them if they know what (or where) osso buco is. (I for one would really like to know.) And if they answer, "No, I don't know how to cut hair," thank them for their honesty, proceed to the next stylist and keep the osso buco to yourself.

Remembering Princess Di

The year 1981 got off to a bad start. President Reagan was shot, the economy was weak, and the world was still dealing with and reeling from the Ayatollah mess.

True, the hostages were home and that was cause for celebration. And then the rumors started to fly about Prince Charles, the celebrated bachelor, and some kindergarten teacher named Diana Spencer. And before you could say "My Fair Lady," the entire globe was invited to watch a nice young girl from Kensington become the Princess of Wales.

In retrospect it seemed like the launching of the '80s, in all its opulence and conspicuous consumption. But from the start, Diana refused to fit the mold of airhead heiress. She had style, yes, but she had heart. She had two sons and she took them to school, not boarding school, but one just around the corner. She made sure they went to McDonald's just like all the other kids, and the supermarket, and the local stationery store. If she wasn't always there with them, it was to protect their privacy, and to avoid the obvious photo opportunity. She was not playing mommy, you see. She really was a good mum.

There's something about the word "princess" that sets the teeth on edge. And yet there was something about Diana that made being a princess a decent sort of thing. Webster defines princess—after the standard royalty stuff—this way: "any woman regarded as like a princess, as in being graceful, accomplished, or outstanding in some way, or, pampered, protected, snobbish, arrogant, etc."

What we loved about Diana was the fact that she fit the first definition, not the second. Sure she was pampered, but she never seemed helpless, either by default or design. Protected? Not hardly. She was always in the camera's glare. Snobbish? Ask any of the AIDS patients she visited in the night, to avoid the media circus. Arrogant? Not by a long shot. If Diana was a literary character she came closer to Anna Karenina than Madame Bovary or even Emma. She was neither saint nor sinner. Like all of us, she did the best she could. And sometimes she did better than the rest of us.

I've never been much of a "royal watcher," but I did set my alarm for 2 a.m. back in July of 1981 so that I, at home in Los Angeles, could see the royal wedding. It was history after all. It was her story too. It turns out to have been the least interesting part of her story, a cautionary tale to all girls (Momma, don't let your babies grow up to be cowboys...or princesses), proof that one's wedding day should not be the best day of one's life. Otherwise it's all downhill from there.

It wasn't all downhill for Diana, though. And the best times for her were probably the times spent with her family and friends and with the countless strangers whose lives she touched and made better by her unselfishness. Not by royal gesture, but human kindness.

Long after the photos and video footage of Diana's hairdos, jewels, and gowns have faded, the legacy of her short life, the good she did to others, will continue to shine. That's what made her truly royal, not her marriage to a prince, but her character.

I'd like to think that my six-year-old daughter is a fledgling Princess Di. Not because she plays dress-up (she rarely does) or wants to marry a prince (she doesn't). But because she wants to volunteer for our town's Meals on Wheels program and give her old toys to hospitals. Those are the kind of things Princess Di would have done and after all is said and done, those are the things—her grace, not just her pretty face—she should be remembered for.

A few things I've noticed

Learning patience, given time

The world, I've decided, is divided into two groups: those of us who arrive on time, and the people who keep us waiting. The first group contains a subset: The people who are early. (Let's face it, if you're going to be on time, why not get there five minutes ahead of schedule?) The people not in this first group are already scratching their heads and saying, "Huh?" They're thinking, "Never mind. I'll read this later." That's just fine; you all find something else to do. This essay is really for the early birds. It'll give you something to read while you're waiting for your group two friends to arrive.

What is it about waiting that is so—how shall I put this, annoying? Is it the waste of time, the edginess it engenders? Or is it just the fact that the people you are waiting for have, unintentionally or not, given you the impression that they think you have nothing better to do? Can you already tell from the tone of this piece that I really hate to be kept waiting? Yes, I'm sure you can. But I digress. This is meant to be a helpful essay. It is not meant to change on-timers into late-arrivers (heaven forefend!). And I'm not so unrealistic as to believe one essay could transform that other group into responsible, punctual citizens. On the other hand, it's worth a shot. So Part 1 will be an impassioned plea for prompt-ness. Part 2, the realistic part, will offer things to do while you're waiting for that friend or family member who's never on time.

Let me begin with a confession. I used to be a tardy person, always running behind the clock. I told myself it was one of my more endearing qualities. It wasn't. It led to people thinking of me as flighty at best, irresponsible at worst. And then I got this flash of insight that said, "If you're early, people will think you like them." And since, as a rule, I usually do, I found it easy to change my non-post-haste ways. Once I made the decision to get there on time no matter what, it became easier until finally it was second nature. Here's the secret. Figure out when you want to arrive, and then count backward from there. Include travel time, pull-yourself-together time and, most important, unforeseeable-events time. Like the mother ship from Mars landing in the HOV lane of the express-way and you getting caught behind the CNN cameras. Then add an extra five minutes and—presto!—Ladies and gentlemen, we have an early bird.

For those of you who already know how to get where you're going on time or better, a few suggestions for how to make the best use of those extra minutes. First of all, don't think it's your mistake, that you've got the wrong date, place, time, planet. Relax. You don't. Don't waste time getting angry, either; it'll ruin your looks and possibly your day. Ditto for feeling self-righteous or superior. Next thing you know, you'll remember, too late, that you forgot to put money in the parking meter, and there you'll be, owing another $10 to the local constabulary. We all have our little shortcomings. So don't rub it in. They're late, you're not. Look at this as a gift of time. Time to, say, make out your Christmas-card list, address the cards, mail the cards. So what if it's July? It's never too soon for holiday cheer. Or come prepared, especially if you're meeting a repeat offender. Bring all that mending you never have time to do. A large tote bag or a smart leather briefcase will carry a passel of undarned socks. And those little sewing kits they sell at hardware stores are so cute. Now you have an excuse to buy one. Or you can carry a notebook and pen and write a curmudgeonly essay on how you hate to be kept waiting. Like I'm doing right now. While I'm waiting for my friend who's always late to arrive. No, not you Denise, someone else.

Actually, I find that being made to wait bothers me a whole lot less now that I'm ten years into my new career, which I guess is not so new any more. The one called being a mother. The one that requires a lot of creative uses of "wait time." Waiting in my car for drop-offs and pickups. (A good time to make up menu plans for the next day/week/month/year.) Waiting for the piano/karate/ballet/swimming lesson to be over. (A good time to catch up on ironing, but it's so hard to find a convenient wall socket when you're not at home.) Then there's my personal favorite: waiting for someone—anyone—to pick up his or her room, clear the table, or get in the car. (A good time to count to 10, slowly.)

I'm sure that someday my kids will be as punctual as their father and I are. (He and I met because we were 60 minutes early for an hourly air shuttle.) But that would mean our children would be all grown up. And there are some things for which I really don't mind waiting.

Funny—you don't sound like a runner

Steven is a funny runner. Now by this I do not mean that his stride is peculiar, or that there is a wiggle in his walk, or that he sometimes goes by the name of Chantilly Lace. No. What I mean is Steven is an extremely funny person who also happens to be an avid user of Nikes, Reeboks, and other shoes affiliated with flying-feet activities.

Before I met Steven, I didn't think this combination was possible in a person. Maybe you'd find a good-humored cheetah joking in the jungle or vamping on the veldt, but a jocular jogger? Forget about it. It seemed to me that people who ran did so with a grim look on their faces and a grimmer outlook on life. Not Steven. He is fleet of foot, quick of wit, and full of joie de vivre. In almost every way imaginable, he's hard to keep up with.

Now me, I'm a stroller. Always have been, although this may have something to do with all the years I spent pushing one (a stroller, that is). Yes, I've seen those baby-jogger contraptions, but frankly they scare me. I like to stop and smell the flowers, taste the Danish, maybe even sit for a while. I enjoy the great outdoors, but at my own pace, which is closer to a snail's than a gazelle's.

But Steven has pointed out to me, without his knowing it, that I'm a snob. I didn't think that humor and exercise went together. Now I know they do. They run or walk hand in hand.

I used to wish those joggers I passed on the road in the morning would smile every once in a while. I'd think smugly to myself that maybe they were just lost in thought, constructing the next bon mot they would inject into polite conversation, just as soon as they stopped panting and sweating.

But recently I've noticed a change in those peppy people who go whizzing past me while I walk: Their demeanor is less meaner. This change coincidently coincided with my change in attitude (hmmm). Once I admitted there was at least the possibility of poetry in motion, I had to allow that there might be levity in motion, too.

The other day I saw two women laughing together as they strode side by side. Maybe it's the time of year here in the Northern Hemisphere, or maybe runners aren't as grumpy as I've been pretending they were. All I know is I can no longer afford the conceit that you can either be funny or in good shape. I've decided to settle for both. I may never run a marathon—did I say "may"? Forgive me, I meant "will." I will never run a marathon, not even if they're handing out free chocolate-chip cookies at the finish line. But I do enjoy a brisk walk, a little aerobic activity, and—dare I say it?—weight lifting (with very light weights). I like doing this on a daily basis. Maybe it's because I spend so much time in my head, every now and then I need to make sure the rest of me still works.

The point is, I'm finally learning we don't have to be one thing or another. We can be a collage.

You can be a working mom who paints (I was going to add "in her spare time," but I don't think working moms have much of that). Or a stay-at-home who plays piano and the stock market, though not at the same time. You can be married or single, have children or not, work in an office, work at home. You can change careers—several times. You can move across the country, move around the world. Or you can stay exactly where you are.

I think all of us are collages, little bits of this and that stuck together over the course of time, resulting in a uniquely beautiful work of art. Or, at the very least, a piece of work.

Think of all the bits of you stuck behind your current form, the bits your kids would never in a million years believe were once you. Would never in a million years believe still are you. Like you playing piccolo in the high school marching band. Or maybe lead guitar in a rock band.

Maybe you used to be a surfer, only now you're a CPA. Stranger things have happened, are happening as we speak. My aforementioned friend Steve is a writer/singer/hiker/father/husband/teacher and a thoughtful, loving wacko. I think he dances, too. A serendipitous life is truly a masterpiece—one that gratefully requires neither painting nor modeling skills. Though if you're lucky enough to have those talents, then I say mazel tov.

Middle Earth or middle school?

This is the story I'm constantly told by media, well-meaning friends, and bestselling experts: My kids have just entered uncharted territory, filled with dark secrets and battles for power and glorious alliances. Groups, factions, mysterious happenings, challenges, and trials—good and evil—collide.

Where are they, Middle Earth? Almost—they've just started middle school. It's a far cry from safe, cozy elementary school. It has lockers and homework, and it's the first time kids are expected to navigate through schedules on their own know-how.

There's an entire section now in every bookstore devoted to dealing with children of middle-school age. Sometimes they're called preadolescent, sometimes they're called tweeners (ouch)—but the refrain is the same: There's trouble ahead. Big trouble.

So I went to my first middle school parents' meeting and found it jammed with mothers wanting to find out what the new year would bring and just how bad they could expect their lives to get dealing with academic and athletic and peer pressures. There was the multipurpose calm-down pep-talk given by the principal and a few teachers.

Then this guy got up—a guidance counselor who could pass for a high-school senior. I sensed even before he opened his mouth that he was going to say something interesting and honest—and he did. He said that seventh or eighth grade is when kids are most likely to get labeled with stereotypes that follow them through high school, if not college and beyond.

His message was that middle school is when kids "lose it"—stop doing homework, try drugs, experiment with sex. And once they "lose it," they can't get it back. They are simply typecast as a loser.

I expected a deafening silence or maybe a blood curdling scream would follow his thought provoking comments, but instead the meeting moved on at that breakneck speed all meetings accelerate to when people don't want to hear unsettling news. But his words stayed with me, making me wonder: What's a mother to do?

So the next day I called up the counselor, thanked him for his candor, and asked the obvious question: What can parents do to keep kids from falling into the antisocial abyss? Can we help them pick a better stereotype? You know, the good-looking popular athlete-genius stereotype? His answer was no. But parents can do three things so simple they're often overlooked.

• Listen to kids. Don't be too quick to offer advice. Let them talk, and talk, and talk. Stop whatever it is you're doing and get interested, even if you're not, and even if they are sharing the most excruciatingly boring part of their day with you—because after they get past all the dull stuff, they might tell you something about the fight that broke out in science class or the kid that threatened to beat them up.

• Praise kids when they do something good—even if it's not a big deal. Don't throw them a party every time they make their bed, but let them know you appreciate their help around the house, or that you're glad they got a 'B' on their math test. Kids who feel good about themselves will do bad things—but not regularly, and if they do, they'll feel bad enough that they don't want to repeat the experience. And hey, they listen to your dull stuff, too.

• Don't push kids. People who are pushed come to depend on some external force, a parent for example, keeping the pressure on them to succeed. Don't follow them around making excuses for them when they mess up. Expect them to do well, accept them when they don't.

Finally the counselor said, think what kind of people you want your kids to become—what are the qualities you want them to live?

Now, four weeks into middle school, I think parents, above all, have to be kids' advocates—not to fight their battles for them, but with them.

The biggest battle I'm seeing may be combating the stereotypes that some teachers and experts have of our children. At our back-to-school night we were handed a list of "characteristics of early adolescents." Any other group would be calling the Anti-Defamation League if they were described in these terms.

According to the list, preadolescents are, among other things: forgetful, self-doubting, peer-oriented, bored by routine and social amenities, resentful of direction and orders, moody, gossipy, extremely loyal to friends, and inclined toward crushes. That describes a lot of adults I know. If we accept these stereotypes without question, does it become self-fulfilling prophesy? I do think this is a battle that can be won—even if part of it is respecting the people who say your kids are going to behave badly and there's nothing you can do about it.

We can all do our part. If we fight to make the world a kinder, gentler place then maybe middle school will follow suit.

Joining the crowd from the 'burbs

When my friend told me my new haircut looked "very suburban" other words that begin with the prefix "sub" immediately sprang to thought. Substandard. Subhuman. Subpoena.

No your Honor, I don't really think one pithy put-down is grounds for a lawsuit. The obvious intent of this verbal clip, however, was that a city haircut is by definition a cut above one snipped in the suburbs. And now that I am officially one of the Bridge and Tunnel people, I've been thinking about the differences between the metro life and the one lived on the outskirts. The only conclusion I've come up with so far is that neither one is better than the other. They're as different as night and day. Some live in the city; others used to.

Mine wasn't so much a case of love it or leave it; it was more like love it and leave it. I loved living in New York right up to the moment that the movers arrived to cart our furniture 28 minutes north. The move was about a growing family, as well as a shrinking ability to cope with the banalities of urban life. It wasn't the noise, the crowds, and the crime. Piece of cake. It was the smaller inconveniences that ballooned out of proportion. You try pushing a stroller through three locked doors, and across eight city blocks to get to the nearest playground—when you're pregnant.

The fact is I was never really a true New Yorker, even though I lived there for five years (which is like 15 years in any other city). I could do a fair imitation of a New Yorker's dress (black pants, black boots, black sweater, black belt), but I never perfected the New York walk, the keep your eyes on the sidewalk in front of you with a sort of glazed look that says I'm not really here. I understood the need for "the look" and the desire for some small shred of privacy when surrounded by 8 million neighbors. But I kept catching myself looking up—at the buildings, the sky, the people passing by who were too busy looking down to notice me. I couldn't help myself. I was interested. I was a born Yahoo, meant to live out of, not in, town.

Do I miss the city? The museums, the theater, the late night dinners? Of course I do. But then I also used to spend a lot of time missing that from our apartment when we were either too tired or too babysitter-less to avail ourselves of such pleasures. Let's face it, cable TV is about the same no matter where you live. And there are so many things about living in the suburbs that fit me like a soft old sneaker, fit the life I'm living now, not the one I used to have, or the one I'll have again someday.

Like having a backyard with a swing. Like driving to the supermarket instead of hauling home as many grocery bags as I could fit on the back of a stroller. Like having neighborhood kids and neighborhood mothers for my kids and me to play with. My husband has a 10-minute walk to the train station, occasionally shared with a fellow commuter. They can talk if they feel like it, or just trudge along in comfortable silence. They can even keep their eyes off the pavement until they reach Grand Central Station.

Don't get me wrong. I'm not saying my life is for everyone. I know there are millions of families who by choice are raising their kids in the urban rather than suburban mode. To them I say more power to you. I chose to follow a yellow brick road that led to a slightly sitcom life. I see myself as a cross between June and Eldridge Cleaver, a sort of "Soul on Ice Cream." I can look up from my computer now and see a squirrel's face in my window; before, it was a pigeon's face.

Both have their good points and their shortcomings. Neither will ever be house guests. But if forced to make a choice I'd rather stare down a vermin with a bushy tale than one with feathers. Maybe if Disney had made a film about cute pigeons, I'd feel differently. But he didn't, so I don't.

The best part for me about living in the 'burbs" is feeling I can relax, that there aren't so many rules to follow. For example, just the other day I took my oldest daughter to lunch and left pennies as part of the tip. The same friend who chided my haircut once chastised me for doing the very same thing in New York City. "New Yorkers don't do that! Do you want everybody to think you're from out of town?" Now I can leave my pennies with impunity. It's just something that we Yahoos do.

Volunteers: we are stardust, we are muddy

My husband's company had signed up to take part in something called New York Cares. It meant volunteering to clean up a park on the first Saturday in May. When the day rolled around I was surprised to learn how few of his co-workers planned to attend. It seems like everyone's got their Saturday plans these days, their weekend homes and soccer practices, not to mention babies and toddlers not compatible with a city clean-up project.

Our kids are in first grade, so they were gung ho to help. Meanwhile their parents were feeling more oh no than gung ho.

Friday night it poured. Maybe the cleanup will be rained out, my husband and I thought, somewhat hopefully. It had been a long week. We had plans Saturday night. What were we thinking? We don't even live in New York City anymore. How typical of my generation, to talk a good fight and then when the roll is called, be nowhere in sight.

Still, I've always been leery of savior behavior. I didn't want my family to be typecast as the well-to-do do-gooders, the suburbanites come to help out the urbanesque. But lately my husband and I have wanted to start doing something more meaningful with our kids than going to the zoo or the mall or a movie.

Having grown up in the Me-Generation, we can't help but feel it would be swell if our kids could grow up in the We-Generation. To accomplish this will mean a lot less time on-line and in-line. More hours spent thinking about and doing for others. Neighbor behavior.

And I can wistfully recall a time, not so long ago, when most everyone connected with my husband's company would have shown up at such a Saturday undertaking, guns blazing. After all, we were the kids who grew up listening to Crosby, Stills and Nash singing "We can change the world, rearrange the world…"

Now too often our thoughts have turned inward. We're over-booked socially and under-fed spiritually. We all have our good excuses, but at the end of the day an excuse is just a reason not to show up.

Saturday came and the weather was right out of the perfect spring morning catalogue. My husband and I loaded up the kids and drove the 15 minutes from our suburb to our assignment—a Harlem senior citizens' park that needed spring cleaning.

There was raking to do, broken glass to pick up, dead leaves to pile, ground to break and turn over. Flowers to be planted. A day's work indeed. The organizers were well organized. We were met with an ample supply of new shovels, rakes, hoes, and dozens of fresh gardening gloves. The woman in charge was gracious and focused. No anxious standing around, no wandering and wondering what to do. The tasks at hand were explained and assigned.

A dozen and a half people had shown up—the young woman at my husband's office who had signed us up, plus two other work place cohorts, and a spouse, as well as other people from other places. One man had come all the way from Brooklyn—Brooklyn to Harlem is about as "you can't get there from here" as it gets.

Someone had brought a boom box and it was pleasantly blasting us with top-40 songs from my childhood—"Heaven Must Have Sent You From Above," "Tears of a Clown," "I Was Made to Love Her," and "Come See About Me."

The park itself was a gem in the midst of flotsam and jetsam, a fauna work of art, assiduously reclaimed by a small group of pragmatic activists determined to make something bigger and better than the usual sound byte on the nightly news. More beautiful, too.

So smack dab in the middle of drug wars and banal urban decay was this park. It was full of trees and it had a gazebo. It was truly a green oasis. Passersby stopped to watch us digging and weeding. They smiled and waved and said thank you. We all agreed there was nothing more satisfying, more unifying than digging in dirt. We all felt blessed to be there.

We were black and white, men and women, young and old, married and single. For the three hours we worked side by side the only colors that mattered were the brown earth, the green leaves, the blue sky. For lunch we were fed some of the best food I've ever eaten. It was made by the mother of the woman organizer. We were asked to write thank you letters to the deli man who provided the cold drinks. It was a veritable festival of kind hearts and good manners.

My husband and I had to leave before the project was finished. We stayed longer than some, less long than others. No one made us feel bad about going. People stayed for as long as they could. You were made to feel good just for showing up at all.

Our kids made us promise we'd all come back again next year. We will. As we drove home across the bridge where the polo grounds used to be I thought of another song of my youth—"Woodstock," by Joni Mitchell. "We are stardust, we are golden, and we've got to get ourselves back to the garden."

We're the rich ones alright, just like everyone else that showed up. We got to spend one Saturday in May making new friends, making something beautiful even better. It doesn't get much richer than that.

A fashionista manifesto that just might fit you

It's hard to make a fashion statement when you don't really speak the language. Try as I might to rock steady on the currents of style, I've been known to have this habit of straying one step beyond. I'll go overboard, sartorially speaking: a brooch too big, a blouse too blouson, a blazer too blazing—you get the picture. There are far worse fates.

Still, it would be nice to get up and get dressed some morning, any morning, and not feel an undeniable angst about facing the closet. This is why I now have my version of a uniform. Name tag not included. These days I rarely vary it. Jeans, white turtleneck tucked in at the waist, brown leather belt, white socks and sneakers, pearl earrings (why not?). My goal is to blend in without looking bland; in short, to have a nice day. Secretly I hope to be mistaken for a college student

But then the other morning it seemed as if all the clothes I saw on me, and everyone else for that matter, were dated. We all looked like we were stuck in the '80s. Oh I'll be kind and say maybe the 90s. The commuters, the house moms, even the happy shopkeepers were out of style across the board, male and female alike. It was weird, different than looking old; it was looking out of it. I sensed that fashion had moved on like a train out of our station, and we were all left standing on the platform of another time, a recent past to be sure, but all the same the past.

Somewhere nearby in New York City, people were dressing au courant. They were of the moment. Not us. We'd lost that fashion feeling. I thought there must be something we can do to fast forward us into the twenty first century. And I think I've come up with a quick-fix fashion manifesto, one that, if followed, will produce immediate results. Notice I didn't say good results. Remember, I'm out of my depth here.

1. Ladies: No more silk scarves over tan trench coats worn over pants ensembles and black low-heeled shoes. The look is too outré, n'est pas? Let's hear it for slickers, bright yellow or green, preferably, over jumpsuits if possible, or maybe a bright blue dress. Shoes? No. Ankle boots? Yes! Also, let's lose as much of the

makeup as we can. It's gone way beyond blotting. Some of us are starting to look positively kabuki.

2. Gentlemen: Stray from gray and head for red. OK, maybe not red, but how about camel? How about robin's-egg blue shirts? How about smiling every now and then?

3. Casual attire: Everyone, and I do mean everyone, in white short-sleeved collared shirts, chinos, and loafers (no socks) forever. There's a difference between dated and timeless. This is a look that looks good on everyone. Tuck the shirt in, or leave it out. Makes no difference to me. Come to think of it, let's all just wear leisure wear all the time. And while we're at it, let's all move to Montecito, California.

Just hanging out with the laundry

Ever since my family and I arrived at our beach rental, I've been hanging our clothing out to dry on the laundry line by the kitchen door. It's a discreet little arrangement, this clothesline and poles, hidden from view by a three-sided fence.

The house stands at the end of a dead-end dirt road that even the indigenous wild rabbits have a hard time finding. We do have enough of them hopping around to keep our dogs perpetually on alert and permanently in the fenced backyard, though. This keeps them far from the madding bunnies, and far from the air and sun drying clean clothes which they'd be only too happy to muddy.

At first I only hung out the towels and sheets. Then I added the shirts because they billow so nicely. But pretty quickly I had every item of clothing, from outer wear to inner sanctum, waving outside in the summer breeze.

Then I started to get interested in the order I hung them in—you know, white shirts with white shorts, bathing suits with bathing suits, chinos with chinos. Dry-goods cliques, so to speak. After that, I got into giving every member of the family her or his own personal row.

It's amazing how quickly a chore can morph into an obsession.

No one seemed to notice at first. My husband was happy that I was saving on the cost of electricity, which we pay for in addition to the rental fee. Our kids liked the way their T-shirts and shorts felt (soft) and smelled (summery). Then last week I thought the line looked so pretty I took a picture of it. Without any children or household pets in the foreground. Or the background, either. Just my laundry. Who do I think I am, David Hockney?

Then this morning I decided to stay home and hang laundry rather than go snorkeling with my husband and kids. A bad sign.

When I finally got down to the beach, I found a clothespin stuck to my bathing suit. I'd absentmindedly pinned it there while hanging the day's master-piece—I mean clean clothes, of course. Plus, I keep trying to work the art of hanging clothes into whatever conversation I am having, with close friends, with total strangers at the food store.

I'm beginning to scare people, I think. They get that wide-eyed look and start to back away slowly, speaking in hushed tones so as not to startle me.

Hey, It's not like I'm obsessing about fabric softener. This is a new/old art form I've discovered, or do I mean stumbled upon? I'm trying to cut back; maybe I'll even use the dryer tomorrow if it rains. But I doubt it. For the time being, I'm hooked.

But let me assure you—let me assure me—that the reason underneath it all is not a desire to be Donna Reed or Betty Crocker or Harriet Nelson. I like hanging laundry because here I have the time to do it.

Back home, on the mainland, I'm the maestro of multitasking. I can keep many appliances going at the same time. The washer, the dryer, the dishwasher, the oven, the computer. I'm a regular one-woman power surge. Time is of the essence every minute of the day.

But here, time means nothing. I've got no deeds to do, no promises to keep. I'm dappled and drowsy and ready to sleep—and in case you didn't notice, I just quoted a line from Simon & Garfunkel's "The 59th Street Bridge Song" (Feelin' Groovy).

Frankly, I'm feeling downright groovy because the one thing I have a lot of at the moment is time. Time to read and write and walk on the beach and listen to music (and listen, really listen, to my children, not just nod and say "uh-huh" because I have a million and 17 things on my mind and 37,000 things to do before bedtime) and yes, even time to hang the laundry out to dry.

This isn't a job that responds well to pressure. You have to have all the time in the world to do it right. That's why I'm so good at it. And because I've discovered this hidden talent heretofore unused, I don't want to share my laundry-hanging ritual with the rest of the family.

Not that anyone's been clamoring to get in on the action. Not that anyone's even more than vaguely noticed that somehow their clothes are always clean in the morning, no matter how sandy and muddy they got the day before. Not that they ever do.

It's magic. It's motherhood. I'm being redundant.

Soon I'll be back home with my machines, and slowly the rush of modern life will take over again. But right now it's turtle time—the tortoise is letting the hare win this race—and me and my flapping clean clothes are feeling just fine.

The drawer: it's a jungle in there

Every home has one, from the smallest studio apartment to the loftiest of mansions. It's called the utility drawer. It's generally found in the kitchen, below the counter space where the phone is. Near, but not near enough, the trash can. It's the last stop on the train that runs from useful item to oblivion. Somehow its contents either never get tossed, or they mysteriously replicate. The things that fill a utility drawer are neither good nor garbage. They belong in that twilight-zone haze of "can't live with 'em, can't live without 'em." Open any utility drawer in America today and here's what you'll find.

1. A sewing kit, without any needles.
2. Six pennies.
3. Several foreign coins of unknown origin.
4. Paper clips.
5. A wooden ruler, broken off diagonally at the 8-inch mark.
6. A calendar, at least two years out of date, with an old schooner and the words "Acme Hardware" emblazoned above it. You can't throw it out because you wrote too many important phone numbers on it when the calendar was still current, and you can't find the time to copy them into your address book, which you lost.
7. Two chewed-up pencils with the nubs worn down. No eraser, either.
8. A small hammer.
9. A domino.
10. A pair of pliers that sticks.
11. One very stale stick of chewing gum, in a pale yellow wrapper.
12. A Phillips head screwdriver with a cracked plastic handle.
13. One gardening glove.
14. A pen that looks dried up but when you try to use it you remember too late that this is the pen that leaks. It has red ink, too.
15. Out-of-date coupons, mixed in with a few still-good ones.
16. A key chain with either a plastic green-haired troll attached to it, or a rubber-ized medallion bearing the phone number of a pizzeria that went out of business.

17. At least seven vaguely familiar-looking keys.
18. A pair of scissors, but not the good pair.

Optional Items (depending on your location—urban, suburban, or rural):

1. One golf ball.
2. Matchbook, with one match left, from "Guido's Gyros and Grinders."
3. A broken red crayon.
4. Package of zinnia seeds.
5. Roll of masking tape.
6. Fishing line.
7. Shoelace.
8. Rubber-band ball.

Now the world would be a perfect place if there were only two kinds of stuff: the stuff that you save, and the stuff that you chuck. But there's that third group, that nebulous nether region of ambiguity. This is the stuff of the utility drawer.

The best thing would be to dump the contents in the nearby trash can and reline the drawer with new shelf paper. But that will never happen. You'll think, "But what if I find the other glove? Maybe those keys really are important. I can't throw out a perfectly good hammer."

And then the phone will ring, you'll grab one of the nubby pencils, faintly scratch down an important phone number on the out-of-date calendar, see an ice-cream coupon that expires today, and run out the door with it, taking one of the mystery keys with you. Maybe it opens the toolbox. Why would anyone put a lock on a toolbox? It'd sure be nice to find the key that opens it. The good ruler's in there, too

Marriage math:
the rhythm of logs

My husband and I are moving the woodpile again. This must be the third time we've done this since the beginning of the year. We move it closer to the house when it's cold outside, farther away when it's warm. Sometimes it's more of a lateral move. Sometimes we just move it for fun. We're trying to find the perfect spot for the whole three cords of it, a place that is both utilitarian and poetic.

Our choices are somewhat limited. The backyard seems best. And no matter how much wood we burn each year, we always seem to have quite a pile of split logs longing to be rearranged.

My husband believes that stacking wood is both a science and an art. I look at the task as a free and mostly pleasant form of exercise, plus an opportunity to commune with nature. I wasn't a child of the '60s, but I was a child in or during the '60s.

The hippie-dippy dopiness of my formative environment may never wear off. I still feel virtuous when I'm doing something outdoors, like moving firewood from one place to another, as opposed to doing something indoors, like shopping. I'll take the dale and the dell over the mall any day.

But my husband should consider writing a book called "The Art of Scientific Wood Piling." I think it would be an instant bestseller, and not just because he's a very good writer. I think he'd strike a resonant chord on the emotional guitar of many men's lives. They may not be star dust, they may never be golden, but—by cracky—they will get themselves back to the garden. (Why do you think they called it Woodstock?)

When I work with my husband in the yard, we rarely speak. It's not a time for chitchat; this much I've learned, in all my years of pretending to be one of the guys. Girls talk, boys grunt and nod. So when I'm moving the woodpile, I act like a registered monk, or a teamster who's taken a vow of silence. I follow directions; I try to make the pile straight. "Build it up!" my husband says (it's the only thing he utters). I used to mutter "duh" under my breath until I noticed that my side of the pile was often crooked and leaning, in a leering sort of way, and that his side wasn't.

His woodpile is always picture perfect—straight, proud, and tall. To him, the wood is not just fuel; it's a walk backward into history, a flight of fancy on solid ground.

I think he also enjoys moving the woodpile because he spends so much time at a desk. In our modern world, we have to invent reasons and ways to stay active. The woodpile is one reason and way.

I shouldn't call it a "pile," come to think of it. It's more like the wall of wood. It stretches almost 50 feet across our property and stands at least four feet tall. It's a monolith, lying down.

I learn a lot about us when I'm engaged in lifting logs. I learn about partnership and cooperation—marriage as an elementary-school project. There's a right way to place the logs and a wrong way, let me tell you. The right way works, the wrong way doesn't. There's arithmetic to making the logs stack steady, and though it takes time to learn it, it's well worth the effort. Just like a lot of things in life.

When I work in the yard with my husband, I learn the math of marriage. The little things we do together, they all add up. The sum of us is more than the logs—of that I'm pretty sure. But when I look at that lovely wall of wood behind our house, I'm reminded that we are partners. We have dreams and aspirations, together and apart. We have children, we have logs, we have love.

That's what the firewood tells me when I wonder if it has found its final resting place. I don't think so. My husband will find a reason to move it come November.

Sometimes I can feel my husband watching me try to wedge a log into a space where it clearly (to him anyway) doesn't belong. Patiently, he'll gesture with his eyebrows that I should reconsider. I used to think, "Sheesh, it's not like we're working on a jigsaw puzzle here." But the longer I do this thing with the woodpile, the more I'm convinced that there is a right place for every log, and several wrong places, too. Recently our son stopped by on his way to the garage. He started to put a log in a rather precarious spot (to me anyway). "Not there," I chided him. "There," I said, pointing to a spot three inches farther down the row. He smiled and acquiesced, although something in the way he looked at me seemed to say, "Whatever."

I look forward to moving the woodpile again. I've learned to enjoy the task, literally and figuratively. It gives me hope and a sense of humble pride. And it gives me a feeling, however fleeting, of work well done. That's worth moving a few hundred logs for, every couple months or so.

Elegy fandango at the Women's Club

I was sitting at my post at the Barclay classes, in the downstairs ballroom of the Bronxville Women's Club when Allison came in. I was serving as hostess for Barclay that night, something we mothers volunteer to do as a way of helping out.

Barclay has been around since the 1930s. It's an old world concept—teaching children how to dance and make polite conversation—that's slightly out of step with planet Internet. It's a beloved anachronism that some of us hold dear. Allison does, I know.

Her son Luke goes to Barclay, with his hair slicked back looking like the junior poster boy for Ralph Lauren. Luke sheepishly admits to liking dance class but that's probably because he almost always wins a prize—even the ones that are given out for silly reasons having nothing to do with the ability to foxtrot. Luke is in his element at Barclay. My son and daughter are not, but they try to make the best of it. They both love to dance, but they are diamonds in the rough. They are nine years old. They are anything but polished.

Allison was standing in the doorway with her daughter Grace, who is five. Allison had just returned from seeing her father, Grace's grandfather, who is dying. He's lived a long, and on balance good life, but who among us will ever be truly ready to go? I don't really know the man, but my guess is that he's not thrilled with this turn of events.

Allison looked bleary and weary. Like most of us in this all too modern world, she juggles far too many things: a full time job, two kids, a husband, and now, caring for a fading parent. So I stood up and gave her a hug, because sometimes hugging is the only thing you can do.

Allison started to cry and then she apologized the way people often do, as if showing grief were impolite. I hugged her again and said crying is the only appropriate response when someone you love is dying. It's bad manners *not* to cry and so cry we must. There are standards to uphold. After all, here we are at the Barclay classes, setting a good example.

The children weren't watching anyway, they were too busy looking at their feet, trying not to step on each other. The other mothers were sitting out of earshot, half watching their children, half catching up on the latest gossip. So Allison and I were safe, unseen. We cried a little more, and then we both started to laugh, which is often the case when you're full of emotion...Something about tears at a cotillion struck us both as funny. One release followed another. Tears, then laughter. Then Kleenex and blotting.

I sat down again, and Allison remained standing, watching her son dance with a girl a good head taller than he was, proud of how he managed to move her across the dance floor, like she was a very important piece of furniture, not to be nicked or scratched.

Little Grace swayed in time to the music, holding on to her mother's hand. And all of a sudden Grace and Allison were dancing together in the hallway, just out of view, where the other children and mothers couldn't see them. The piano player purred a version of "Strangers in the Night", while the drummer kept time with his brushes on the cymbal and snare. Allison and Grace took turns twirling each other, gliding and two stepping lightly back and forth. Across the room Luke was still dancing; across town at the hospice, Allison's father was still dying. Nothing had changed, and yet everything was different. The gift of Grace, I thought to myself. Allison has the gift of Grace.

This beautiful child, a cherub in pigtails and overalls, unaware of her mother's sorrow, had lifted her out of it, with what? With dancing. It was a perfectly natural, spontaneous reaction to the music. That's what made it so right and not the least bit surreal. There was nothing left to do but dance. So that's what Allison did. For that very brief time she was completely unconscious of her surroundings; she didn't know that I was watching. She wasn't dancing for effect. It was just one of those private moments, as common as a miracle, she was sharing with her daughter and herself. And I had the privilege of bearing witness to it. The only one who would have loved it more was Allison's father. And since he couldn't be there, someone had to watch it for him. Lucky for me, it was me. Allison was graceful and Grace was idyllic. Together they were poetry in motion. It wasn't an elegy exactly. But it was lyrical, transcendent.

Unbroken connection

I will never forget what a beautiful day it started out to be. Sunny, bright, and clear, a day that begged you to stay outside. And so I did, even though I usually go straight home after dropping off the kids at school. But that Tuesday felt special, so I jogged around the quarter-mile track for half an hour, grateful for the morning, then did a few errands that were in walking distance from my car, just to extend the moment.

At 8:45, I used my cell phone to call home and check for messages. There weren't any. Just before 9 o'clock, I was driving up the hill to my house. I turned on the radio and heard about a plane crashing into the World Trade Center. I pulled into the driveway as the man on NPR was saying that details were sketchy.

I went inside and saw I had two messages, one at 8:48, one at 8:53, both from my husband. He said that he was all right, but the World Trade Center was on fire, and that I should pray. The second call, five minutes later, was a request that I call my mom to ask her to pray. I almost didn't recognize his voice. I called my mom, and told her what I knew. I almost didn't recognize my own voice.

I ran upstairs and turned on the TV, just in time to see the second plane fly straight into the second tower. The newscaster didn't even know it was happening behind her. All this time, I was also trying to reach my husband by phone, but all I got was that rapid busy signal that tells you something is wrong.

My husband works two blocks from what is now known as ground zero. His 59th-floor office gives him a panoramic view of both rivers, all the bridges, and—on that morning for the last time—the twin towers. I called his cell phone; same problem. No calls were getting through. I called the main number at his firm. I called his private line. I prayed.

Finally, I thought "I'll send an e-mail—it's a message in a bottle at best, but maybe somehow he'll get it." I told him I was praying. I told him to come home.

My husband has something called a Blackberry. It's a hand-held device that can send and receive e-mail. I love his Blackberry. I always have; it allows him to stay in touch with his office while remaining on vacation. I love it even more now. He had it with him that morning. He took it with him when he evacuated his office.

At 9:30, he e-mailed me that he was all right and was driving home with a woman from his office who lives one town away from us. I knew he was no longer in his building, but I didn't know anything else. He kept e-mailing me that he was OK.

Then the first building fell. Then his mother called. I told her he was all right, but still downtown. He was trying to drive home. Then I heard all the roads were closed.

The phone rang; it was him. He was in his car, but before he could tell me where he was, we got cut off.

A friend of mine showed up at the door with her 18-month-old son. I told her I had just gotten a call from my husband, but I didn't know where he was. She said she wanted to stay with me. I told her that would be great.

We both saw the second tower collapse. Her little boy didn't—he was happily playing with some toys he had found. We kept him away from the TV set. I checked my e-mail for some new word. Nothing. Nothing. Nothing for the longest 15 minutes of my life.

Then a message that he was safe in a parking lot on the Lower East Side, trying to get on FDR Drive.

My friend went home. I turned off the TV and prayed. Just prayed. Nothing directed or fancy, just "God God God." At 11 o'clock, still morning, though time now felt like granite, the phone rang again. It was him. He said, "You know I always call you when I'm 20 minutes away."

He told me to go get the kids. I said, "Funny enough, I'm bringing them home for lunch today. I'm picking them up in 30 minutes." I was trying to sound almost casual, so emotion wouldn't get the best of me.

He said, "Go get them now." He had just driven through a war zone. His was probably one of the last cars to get out of the city that day. He needed to see his children.

I couldn't begin to comprehend what he'd just been through, what he'd seen or how he felt. But I understood that life had changed, and I went to the school.

I called my mother before I left. She lives five minutes away. I told her what I was doing and asked her to come over. I said, "I don't want him to come home to an empty house. Just in case I got stuck at school, or in traffic. Just in case."

We live in a commuter town, 30 minutes from Grand Central Station. Many people work in the city. Many parents work downtown. I was worried about what I'd find at the school—panic, confusion, fear?

Instead, I found calm and order. Also disbelief and shock, but muted.

I asked a friend of mine—a second-grade teacher, a mother—if she thought it would be ok for me to get my children out of their classrooms early. She said, "Go ahead. Other parents have already been here. Take your kids home."

I walked into my son's class, and found them all working quietly. His teacher told me they knew something was going on, that the World Trade Center was burning. Other parents had already been there to take their children home. The word "terrorists" wasn't mentioned.

I told my son that everything was fine, I just wanted to pick him up early. I told his teacher he wouldn't be back after lunch. We both acted as if this was just a normal day, except for the fact that the world was falling apart.

Then we went to get his sister. Her class was also calmly at work. They didn't know anything about what was going on. Their teacher did, but had kept it from them. No need to get them upset.

I told my daughter I was taking her home a few minutes early. She wanted to know why.

I said, "I'll tell you when we get in the car."

"Is everything OK?" she asked me.

"Daddy's fine," I said.

We drove the few blocks past the school and turned onto our street. At the bottom of our hill is a traffic light. Our light was red. I looked to my left and saw my husband, in his car, waiting to make the turn up our hill. He saw me, too.

I wanted to jump out of my car and run over to him. But I didn't because I knew I had to act as though it was just an ordinary day. For his sake, for our children's sake. For the world's sake.

I gave him the thumbs-up sign. He gave it back to me. He turned as the light changed. I followed him home. We drove up the hill together.

The comfort of astronomy

September 12, 13, and 14 were days lived in slow motion. I remember making meals, taking the kids to school, trying to act as if. As if, somehow, someway everything would be alright again. My husband worked from home those days, unable to get downtown to his office, cordoned off as it was, two blocks from Ground Zero. He spent most of the time on the phone with his co-workers, making sure everyone was first alive, then alright. Gratefully alive was easy. Everyone was accounted for by the end of September 12th. Alright was trickier. Alright would take some time, especially for those like my husband who had seen the planes, heard the explosions, felt the world coming to an end in an instant. But the world hadn't ended; it just seemed like it had. So he was also trying, almost by rote, like his other partners, dazed and on their phones at their homes, to keep their business from grinding to a halt. Work as therapy, work as a way to keep breathing. Amazingly enough, even in the immediate aftermath of 9/11, clients were calling, insistent as ever. It was almost a relief, I suppose, that for some, the grief and the disbelief were secondary to the business at hand. And the business at hand was business as usual, or at least a ragged approximation thereof.

Every afternoon those first three days we took long walks with our kids. By the river that runs through the outskirts of our town. We had lots of company. Every commuter man and woman was land locked at home. There was no going into New York City. Not for those first few days. You couldn't buy a Wall Street Journal anywhere. Our kids were so relieved to see so much of their dad that they probably coped better than we did. If we were alright, they were alright or so they unconsciously reasoned. So we pretended to be alright.

But by Saturday night the strain of it all, the senselessness and insanity was making them both testy and tearful and argumentative, snapping at each other for reasons they couldn't begin to understand. We'd gone one hour north to our weekend home to try to get some perspective, if not psychically then at least physically. I was tempted to simply send them to bed but my husband had a better idea. He hustled us all outdoors. He piled us all into our oversized, free standing hammock and said, "Now look at that," and then he pointed up at the night sky. And there it was—the universe. Still there. Untouched, unfazed, unbroken.

For the longest time it held our gaze and we said nothing, in awe of the stillness and beauty of it all. Then gradually we began to point out the familiar constellations. There's the Big Dipper and the Little Dipper too. Isn't that? Yes, and look! You can see the Milky Way too.

Then the stars stood out to us. Vega, Altair, Deneb and Arcturus. And finally the red planet Mars.

There was something so comforting about knowing their names. It made them seem, not like abstract sparkles, or distant hot gases or particles of matter, but friends, old friends, reliable and true. Verging on eternal. Unending.

I looked over in the darkness at our children's faces. They were tired, but peaceful again. And they had a little bit of the look of wow in their eyes. (Look how old those stars are; think how long they've been around. Look how small and young we are. Wow.)

The only sound was crickets and the four of us breathing, slow and steady. Together. After a very long time, but not too long, not at all too long, we got up and went back inside. Kissed good night and slept like babies for the first time since September 10th.

0-595-31416-3

Printed in the United States
20867LVS00003B/463-465

9 780595 314164